THE MISSION OF THE CHURCH

James E. Carter

BROADMAN PRESS
Nashville, Tennessee

© Copyright 1974 · Broadman Press
All rights reserved
4285–09
ISBN: 0–8054–8509–0

Library of Congress Catalog Card Number: 73–83832
Dewey Decimal Classification: 262
Printed in the United States of America

Dedicated to
Craig, Keith, and Chyrisse
my children

Preface

Christ's mission is the church's mission. As Jesus Christ came into the world to reveal God and to redeem men, the church is to serve as a channel of God's revelation and as a proclaimer of redemption.

The church is central to God's redemptive plan. This is the institution that has extended the meaning of Christ's life into the world of today.

This book seeks to examine the mission of the church from a biblical standpoint. Too often missions has been too narrowly defined. In seeking to understand the church's mission we can also understand a great deal more about missions. The church is always on mission for God in the world.

Originally this material was prepared as a twelve-part Bible study for *Royal Service*. Grateful appreciation is expressed to Rosanne Osborne, who was then editor of *Royal Service,* and Adrianne Bonham, supervisor, adult department of the Woman's Missionary Union, Auxiliary to the Southern Baptist Convention, for permission to publish this material in this form. Mrs. Ann Maynor and Mrs. Sheila Jones typed the original material. Mrs. Carolyn Lee prepared the final typed copy. For the help of these capable secretaries I am also grateful.

I trust that this book will aid in the understanding and appreciation of the mission of the church. In accepting this mission I would trust, then, that Christ's mission would indeed become our mission in a new and renewed sense.

Contents

1.
The Church:
Made for Mission
Matthew 16:13–20

William Barclay has passed on an account of a man in India who came to an Indian pastor pleading to be allowed to become a member of the church. The pastor knew that this man had no previous connection with the church and that he had not received any previous instruction in the faith from the church. So naturally he wanted to be certain that the man knew what he was doing.

"Tell me," he said, "why you are so anxious to become a member of the church."

The man answered: "By chance there came into my hands a copy of Luke's Gospel. I read it and I thought that I had never heard of anyone so wise and wonderful as Jesus, and I wished to take him as my Master and my Lord. But at that stage I thought that it was simply a matter between him and me and no one else. Then by chance I got a copy of the book of the Acts. Here was a difference. Luke was all about what Jesus said and did. But at the end of Luke, Jesus ascends to his Father, and The Acts begins with the same story. In The Acts, Jesus is no more on earth in the flesh. The Acts is not so much about what Jesus said and did as it is about what Peter and Paul said and did, and above all, about what the church said and did. So," said the man, "I felt I must become a member of that church *which carries on the life of Christ.*"[1]

Simply put, this is the mission of the church: to carry on the life of Jesus Christ in this world.

Jesus came into this world for a redemptive purpose. He was

to reveal God to men and to redeem men from sin. The responsibility of the church is to show God to men and to present the redemptive message of Jesus Christ.

The church was made for mission. When Jesus gathered a group of people who were committed to him, he committed to them a mission.

A basic biblical passage dealing with the origin of the church is found in Matthew 16:13–20. Inherent in the very foundation of the church is its mission.

Founder

As Jesus and his followers were in the area of Caesarea Philippi, he asked them an apparently simple question: "Whom do men say that I the Son of man am?" (Matt. 16:13). On the answer would turn their understanding of both Jesus' person and purpose.

They replied with the answers they had overheard. But general answers never satisfy the questions about Jesus. When he directed the question to them, a personal decision was demanded.

Simon Peter answered, "Thou art the Christ, the Son of the living God" (Matt. 16:16). In this answer he affirmed that Jesus was the long-awaited Messiah. ("Christ" is the Greek word that corresponds to the Hebrew "Messiah.") And he also affirmed that Jesus was the Son of God.

The place where this confession was made is significant. The worship of Baal had once been quite active in the area. Close to Caesarea was a cavern said to be the birthplace of Pan, the Greek god of nature. The source of the Jordan River, deeply embedded in Jewish history, was there. And in the city of Caesarea Philippi was a temple built to the godhead of Caesar. Against the background of world religions, Jesus demanded the disciples' verdict of him.

The founder of the church is Jesus Christ. It is Christ that makes the church different from any other movement, organization, or society. Even though composed of persons, organized for work, and gathered by choice, the church is distinct from any other society because of the presence and the purpose of Christ. Christian faith consists in knowing Christ.

Foundation

Jesus was pleased with Peter's answer. He indicated that this was not an insight that could come from either human observation or instruction. God had enabled Peter to understand the identity and the intention of Jesus.

Jesus replied, "Thou art Peter, and upon this rock I will build my church" (Matt. 16:18).

Around this statement many controversies and divergent interpretations have raged. Jesus referred to the nickname that he had given to Simon, the son of John. He called him Peter, a rock. A rock is often used as a foundation.

Some have thought that Peter himself was the rock, the foundation, upon which Jesus built his church. Others have considered it to be the truth that Peter had expressed: that Jesus was the Christ. The faith of Peter is one possibility. Since there is obviously a play on the words "Peter" and "rock," Jesus could have meant that Peter was one rock that would be used as a building stone on the foundation stone, Jesus Christ himself.

In 2 Corinthians 3:11 Paul declared: "For other foundation can no man lay than that which is laid, which is Jesus Christ." Reference is made in Ephesians 2:20 to Jesus Christ being the chief cornerstone and to the believers being built upon that stone into a temple of God. Peter, himself, had a reference to the foundation and building stones in 2 Peter 2:4.

Jesus must be the foundation upon which the church is built. Upon that foundation a person who recognizes Jesus as the Christ places his life. As stones placed on a foundation, Christians comprise the church which belongs to Christ. Through Peter and all others who would accept him, Christ could build his church.

Features

Notice that Jesus called it "my" church. The church belongs to Jesus Christ. If the church is the body of Christ, a metaphor used to describe it, then it must belong to Christ, the head. It also must be responsive to Christ.

The church is also in the process of being built. It is ever becoming. Jesus builds his church from those who come to him in the confession of faith. These people have come at different times and at various places. From them he has built a church.

Since Jesus Christ builds the church, he will determine its essential character. The church must be so sensitive to Christ and to his direction that it assumes the shape he wants it to take. At times it may have different forms; it may need to go in new directions; untried and unproven approaches to its mission and ministry may have to be attempted.

One church has recently completed a "live-in" renovation of its worship center. The pastor observed that it was rather disconcerting to worship in an unfinished church. Then he realized that this is always the character of the church as built by Jesus Christ: it is unfinished. The finished churches have frozen doctrines into creeds, locked worship into ritual and liturgy, and confined the Holy Spirit to certain forms. As the church is built by Jesus Christ, it is capable of being built in the fashion that he intends. This is what makes the church a living organism. The organization is not the church. The living organism that responds to Christ is the church.

Interestingly enough, the word "church" appears only twice in the Gospels. It is found in Matthew 16:18 and in Matthew 18:17. The English word "church" is used to translate a Greek word that has as its basic meaning "called out." It was used for an assembly, or a group, called for a purpose. It is not essentially a religious word. It was sometimes used for political assemblies, civic assemblies, or social assemblies. In the Greek translation of the Old Testament this word was used to describe the congregation of Israel, the people of God. In the Hebrew usage it was a religious assembly.

The very word, then, implies a feature of the church: it is a group of people called out by God through Jesus Christ. Baptists have believed that the church is a "gathered" church. By this it is meant that people who become members of the church, who become the church, are gathered by the common experience of salvation through faith in Jesus Christ.

It becomes obvious that the church is a community; it is a community of faith. Jesus called those who were his first disciples. They became a community of persons who responded to his call. Twelve disciples were chosen. This was reminiscent of the twelve tribes of Israel. The common tie which binds all people who compose the church is faith in Jesus Christ and personal commitment to him. So the church is a community of faith called by Jesus Christ composed of those persons who respond in faith to his summons. The head of the church is Christ; it responds to his will and is empowered by his Holy Spirit.

Should we speak of the church or of churches? Is the church only a local assembly of people gathered in the name of Christ, or is it also a universal company of believers throughout all time and in all places who have responded to Christ's call?

Actually the church is known both universally and locally. At times the church has been considered only in terms of the local church. But the community of faith is larger than the local church. However, the community of faith is known in a particular locality by the local church. The work of the church in a given locality is done by a local church or it is not done at all. The mission of the church is carried out by local churches or it is not carried out at all.

The New Testament refers to both local churches and to the church in a universal sense. For instance, Paul wrote a letter to "the church of God which is at Corinth" (1 Cor. 1:2). But in Ephesians 3:10 he obviously is referring to a church that is more than local. The cause of Christ in its widest sense goes beyond a particular spot. The invisible church is seen in the visible, local church.

The acceptance of mission must be a feature of the church. Jesus was recognized by Peter as the Messiah. The Messiah had a mission in the world. If the church is the community of faith, chosen, headed, and empowered by the Messiah, then the mission of the Messiah becomes the mission of the church.

Future

The church has a great future. Since the church has been founded by Jesus Christ and has been built both by him and upon him, its future rests in him. Believing that the church was no accidental occurrence but rather the intention of Jesus, we can believe that the church will not only survive but will serve in the future.

Something of the future of the church is expressed in another statement made by Jesus to Peter: "and the gates of hell shall not prevail against it" (Matt. 16:18).

The identification of the "gates of hell" has sometimes given trouble. The RSV translates this statement as "the powers of death." J. B. Phillips follows this. *The New English Bible* (1961) words it a little differently but continues the same idea: "the forces of death shall never overpower it."

Actually the word translated "hell" is "hades." In biblical thought "hades" means the place of the dead. So the more modern translations convey the idea that the power of death, as strong as it is, shall never overpower the church.

Many centuries have passed since Jesus made that statement.

Many believers have died during that time. Yet the church has not died. The force of death has not been strong enough to overcome the force of God's love in Jesus Christ as expressed in those who know Jesus Christ by faith.

Christ's church has lived through many political and social revolutions. It has been planted and has grown in many different social and cultural settings. Among the nations of the world it has found a home. The church has lived and will continue to live. It has a future.

The future of the church helps to form the basis for the mission of the church. Since the church is the expression of Christ's mission in the world, it must go on through all time. As long as the world stands, the church has a mission. The future of the church determines the necessity of mission. Without mission there would be no future. Without the future there could be no mission.

Mission may take varying forms. It may be the people sent into other countries and to other people to carry the redemptive message. Missions may be a church attempting to show the love of God in a local situation. Missions may be the churches extending their reach to other parts of the home country and touching disadvantaged, or displaced, or distraught people.

The future of the church gives the assurance that even though all the effects of mission may not be known at a particular time, God's purposes move on. When an act of mission is done, the results may not be immediately obvious. In fact, the search for observable results could obscure the basic thrust of mission. Missions is the investment that is made in the future of the church.

Function

The function of the church shows that it was made for mission. Jesus gave expression to this when he remarked to Peter: "I will give unto thee the keys of the kingdom of heaven: and whatsoever thou shalt bind on earth shall be bound in heaven: and whatsoever thou shalt loose on earth shall be loosed in heaven" (Matt. 16:19).

Keys are symbols of authority and power. The one holding the keys of the kingdom has the ability to provide entrance into the kingdom of heaven. It is not thought that the ability to provide entrance into the kingdom of heaven rests in Peter himself. This is the function of the church in the pursuit of its mission.

The verb form in the original language could be translated to read "that which you bind on earth shall have already been bound in heaven" and "that which you loose on earth shall have been already loosed in heaven." This would indicate that what is done on earth is in accordance with the will of God in heaven. In the *Broadman Bible Commentary* Frank Stagg commented, "This would suggest not that the action on earth would be ratified in heaven but that it is anticipated in heaven. In other words, earth thus follows heaven, not the reverse." [3]

But what are the keys? Peter had confessed that Jesus was the Christ. Christ had responded favorably. So we must conclude that the keys to the kingdom of heaven are identified with the confession of faith in Jesus as the Christ. The one who confesses Jesus as the Son of God and his Savior becomes a citizen of God's kingdom; the one who does not make that confession does not find entrance into the kingdom of heaven.

The church is given the responsibility to make that message known. By living out the redemptive life of Christ and by giving out the redemptive message of Christ it has the ability to bring people into the kingdom of heaven. Similarly, if it fails in that mission, people are denied entrance into God's kingdom. The function of the church is to be true to its redemptive mission.

Jesus warned his disciples not to spread this word. He would have been swarmed by people with distorted ideas of the Messiah and the messianic mission. His opportune time had not yet arrived. When it came, when he was crucified and then resurrected, the message could be known. Then, too, the nature of his messiahship would be known.

But he has not warned his present followers to guard the message. Instead, he has given the present believers the commission to proclaim the message.

Wherever the church expresses its mission, the message of redemption in Jesus Christ is made known. Whether in foreign lands or in the homeland, whether to disadvantaged people or to overadvantaged people, whether through rescue missions or in mission churches, whether in church extension or in related activities, the function of the church in expressing the redemptive message must be considered.

The church was made for mission. When Jesus first began to call those people who would be his expression of the people of God, a community of faith was being formed. Throughout it all mission was in its very life. Each church must accept the mission of the church as its mission.

2.
Empowered for Mission

Acts 2:1–47

In November, 1965, the nation was shocked by a gigantic power failure in the northeastern section of the United States. That whole section of the country was suddenly plunged into darkness. It had everything necessary for electrical power: sources of power, transformers, wires, electrical receptacles, appliances, switches, light bulbs. It had everything necessary for electrical power—except the power.

As churches prepare for mission, they may find themselves in the same situation. They may have everything necessary for mission: motivation, methods, means, and manpower. They may have everything necessary for mission—except power.

The power for mission is from the Holy Spirit. It is the Spirit of God that empowers for mission. We cannot presume to carry out the mission of the church without the power of God at work in the life of the church.

The early church was empowered for mission. The empowering came at the day of Pentecost when the Holy Spirit was poured out in power upon the believers. The exciting story of this event is told in Acts 2.

We must be certain that while the church understands its mission and works at its mission, it also has the power for mission. From a study of the Pentecostal experience we can know something more about the empowerings for mission of the early church and the source of power for the contemporary church. There can never be mission without the power for mission.

Manifestation

The Feast of Pentecost was one of the major Jewish feasts. It fell on the fiftieth day (Pentecost means fiftieth in Greek) after the Passover sabbath. It was a week of weeks after the Passover. Thus it was sometimes called the Feast of Weeks.

Pentecost had an agricultural significance. At the Passover the first of the barley crop was offered as a sacrifice to God. The barley harvest began then. At Pentecost the harvest had been completed; loaves were offered in sacrifice to express gratitude to God for the completed harvest. It also had a religious and historical significance. It commemorated the giving of the Law to Moses on Mount Sinai. It normally was a festive occasion and many people were in Jerusalem for the Feast of Pentecost.

The Christians were together on this Pentecost. Probably it was at some place in the Temple area although some think they might have been in the upper room again.

Suddenly they were aware of strange phenomena: the sound "as of a rushing mighty wind" and the sight of tongues "like as of fire." And they began to speak in tongues foreign to them. Their utterances were prophetic utterances, messages from God about God. They were conscious of being filled by the Holy Spirit.

Many Jewish people from other parts of the world had come to Jerusalem for Pentecost. They heard the gospel in their own language.

There were two explanations: mystery ("What meaneth this?") or mastery ("These men are full of new wine."). Either something was going on that they could not explain or these people were simply drunk.

Apparently the sound of the wind and the symbol of fiery tongues were not seen by the people. This was experienced only by the believers. These were symbols of God's power and his purpose. In the power of God they were to witness to all the people of the world.

The tongues in which these people spoke were tongues unknown to them, not unknown tongues. The dispersed Jews from various parts of the world were able to understand the language in which these people spoke. It was for the purpose of communicating the gospel.

This experience did not mark the coming of the Holy Spirit into the world. Mentions of God's Spirit are made in the Old Testament and in the Gospel accounts. There is a difference after Pentecost, however. In the Old Testament the Holy Spirit seems to be selective and spasmodic. We read of the Spirit coming on a certain person for a purpose. After the day of Pentecost the Holy Spirit is continuous and controlling. The Holy Spirit abides in the life of the believer making constant contact in leading him to the will of God and in the work of God.

That the coming of the Holy Spirit in a manifestation of power had the purpose of mission is seen in the actions of the believers. They did not remain where they were simply enjoying the experience. They went out to the people, witnessing of Christ. God's Spirit has the purpose of thrusting his people out into mission.

Will Pentecost be repeated? Not in the same way. While there will be experiences of the presence and the power of the Holy Spirit, there will not be a reenactment of the day of Pentecost. This was for a particular purpose in the life of the early church. Someone has remarked that oil wells often blow in; they sometimes come in with a great burst of power, spewing of oil, and leaping flames. Later the oil will be pumped into pipes and refineries and to its final destination. There is no need to go back to the spectacular display to know that the oil is there. Similarly, on the day of Pentecost the Holy Spirit came in mighty manifestation. We do not have to have the same manifestations to know of the presence and the power of the Holy Spirit.

Message

Simon Peter gave an explanation of what had happened to the crowd. Their strange behavior was not due to drunkenness. But the significant reason was that they had been filled with God's Spirit.

Taking his text from Joel 2:28–32, Peter showed that God had declared that in the "last days" he would send his Spirit indiscriminately upon the people. It would be accompanied by amazing physical phenomena and would result in the people calling upon the Lord for salvation. Peter was convinced that the time had then arrived. In Jesus Christ God had acted decisively. His Spirit had been poured out on the people. Salvation was available by calling upon the name of the Lord. That to which the prophets looked had been fulfilled in Christ.

Turning from explanation (vv. 14–21), Peter then began a proclamation (vv. 22–36). What he proclaimed was the gospel.

The gospel is the good news that God has acted in Jesus Christ. It is in fulfillment of God's promises. God came into the world in Jesus. He showed his will and his love through Jesus' life. Jesus died on the cross for our sins. But the grave could not hold him. He was raised from the dead. Any who believes him can be saved.

Notice that Peter's proclamation centered on the historic facts of the life of Christ. The good news of the gospel is based on fact, not fancy. It finds its source as well as its content in Jesus Christ. Quoting liberally from various psalms, Peter proclaimed Jesus to the crowd.

His crowning statement was that the Jesus whom they had helped to crucify was both Lord and Christ. He was the Christ, the promised, anointed one of God. And he was Lord, the sovereign ruler over the hearts of men. In calling Jesus Lord, Peter applied to him a name that had previously been used only for God.

The two elements of explanation and proclamation must always be present when the message of Christ is presented. Without the explanation, what is being proclaimed cannot be understood. Without proclamation, the explanation cannot be applied to life.

In the mission actions of a church these two elements are present. In both word and deed the meaning of the life of Christ is applied to human lives. At times the explanation may be more prominent. Someone may ask why interest is shown in that person, why that particular activity is being carried on at that place, or why one would leave his own home and his own interests to serve in that way. An explanation could be given. It is not because of self-interest, nor a desire to be seen, nor a desire to be known. It is because one has been touched by the Holy Spirit of God and both inspired and empowered to serve in his name.

At other times proclamation would be the dominant element. The story of Christ and its application to the life could be made. It may be mute: simply the distribution of tracts, Bibles or Scripture portions, or verses of Scripture placed in the garments that are distributed. At other times it may be in a preaching session. It could, and should often, be in the witnessing experiences. One person could share with another person the meaning of Christ to his life. Many opportunities for proclamation arise in teaching. For example, in teaching illiterates to read, the subject matter could center in the story of Christ.

Whatever is done in mission action, it should not get far from the message. This message may not be overtly presented each time. Surely it would not be crammed down the throats of others. But it is always there, giving an explanation for mission action and providing the content of mission proclamation.

Mission

Simon Peter's message produced amazing results. From the results of this message and the subsequent activities of the believers, we can see something of our mission in the world. Mission action gets its impulse as well as its power from the activity of the Holy Spirit moving through the church.

Salvation. The immediate result was the salvation of three thousand people. This was the most obvious result from the message itself. The salvation of persons is always a major mission interest. What is done in mission has as its basic purpose the salvation of the lost.

The hearers were so convicted by Peter's sermon that they cried out, "Brethren, what shall we do?" (Acts 2:37, RSV).

Peter's reply was simple: repent and believe. Now the form in which the reply has come to us is not quite so simple. In fact, Acts 2:38 has caused some problem in interpretation. C. B. Williams in *The New Testament, a Translation in the Language of the People* translated it: "You must repent—and, as an expression of it, let everyone of you be baptized in the name of Jesus Christ—that you may have your sins forgiven; and then you will receive the gift of the Holy Spirit."

From the total testimony of the New Testament we know that baptism itself does not bring the forgiveness of sins and the gift of the Holy Spirit. Therefore, it is safe to say that Peter was telling them to repent. And on the basis of their repentance, because they had repented, they were to be baptized. Those who had repented and believed would receive the Holy Spirit who was so much in evidence that day.

Notice, too, that Peter asserted that the promise of forgiveness and the presence of the Holy Spirit was inclusive. It applied to those who were near and to those who were far off, to those who were present then and to future descendents, to those who were close to God and to those who were then far from God. All who knew the call of God could know forgiveness and the power of the Holy Spirit.

This promise is the promise that gives meaning to missions. No matter where we go, we know that the people there can be brought to God. There is no place so primitive nor so isolated that God's Spirit cannot reach it to touch the people there. Look at a Foreign Mission Board map and you will notice that the mission impulse has caused the gospel thrust to carry people to new countries and to old countries, to metropolitan areas and to isolated areas, to sophisticated people and to primitive people. And the missionaries go with that promise upon their hearts: that no one is beyond the reach of God.

Enlistment. The people who were touched for God were enlisted for God and his service. That day about three thousand people were added to the Christian fellowship (v. 41).

Enlistment is important. People are not reached for Christ and left to fend for themselves among all the pressures of the world. They are enlisted for fellowship, for nurture, for Christian growth, and for service.

This is one very important element in mission action being conducted by churches. When people are won to Christ, they are enlisted into a fellowship of believers. In this fellowship of believers they can begin to grow and to serve.

It is for this very reason that the primary mission organization is a local church. In either a foreign nation or in a "pioneer" area of the United States, a first step in mission activity is to form a church, whether it is a mission, a chapel, a home fellowship, or an organized church. Something to which the believers can tie is essential for continued ministry. The pattern was established early in Christian life. Churches were established all over the Mediterranean world. This is an essential pattern.

Fellowship. Fellowship was an important part of life of these early Christians. Several aspects of their fellowship are presented in the account in Acts 2.

They studied together. We are told that they "devoted themselves to the apostles' teaching" (v. 42). We cannot learn and grow as Christians unless we study. We study the Bible in Sunday

Schools, in Bible study groups, and in small groups. A knowledge of the Word of God is necessary for both Christian growth and Christian mission.

The early Christians also ate together. The fellowship around a table is one of the most intimate forms of fellowship. At times we have defined fellowship too narrowly and have almost limited it to eating and partying. But eating together is a part of fellowship. These Christians had such a close common bond that they shared their food. The "breaking of bread" is sometimes used to refer to the Lord's Supper. Likely it is not meant in that technical sense here. However, each meal took on spiritual overtones because of the depth of their fellowship.

Sharing together is a part of the Christian fellowship. In verse 45 it is clear that many of them sold their belongings in order to share with other Christians. Apparently this was a voluntary action. Out of their compassion and concern for one another they were willing to share their material goods with one another.

Sharing is at the heart of Christian mission. Whether it is the proclamation of a missionary evangelist or the work of a community center volunteer, sharing is involved. Both spiritually and physically we share what we have.

Worshiping together is essential to Christian fellowship. At this time Jesus' followers had not separated themselves from the Temple worship. In addition to the times of prayer at the Temple they apparently had worship together. So filled were they with the Spirit of Christ that they offered prayer and praise to him continually.

Blessing. Through it all they were able to know the blessing of God. By their life and ministry they were able to attract many others to belief in Christ.

The strength of Christian fellowship and the clarity of Christian witness both combine to bring people to Christ.

The power of God's Holy Spirit was not only known to them in a great outburst on the day of Pentecost. It was also felt by them continually in the days that followed. Because we may not have experienced the Pentecostal outpouring does not mean that we do not possess the Holy Spirit. Day by day, in witness and in fellowship the Holy Spirit is making his presence and his power known.

The mission of the church is a tremendous mission. To properly execute it the power of the Holy Spirit must be known. God has promised his Spirit of power. We cannot make his mission our mission without it.

One of the feats of Hercules was to clean the stables of Augeas. In these stables Augeas had stabled three thousand head of oxen for thirty years and had never cleaned them. It was the task of Hercules to clear away this vast accumulation of filth. He did not even attempt to do it himself. He deflected the course of two rivers so that they flowed through the stables. Their cleansing tide did what no human effort could have done.

The Holy Spirit connects us with a power far beyond ourselves. Through his power we can do things we could never do by ourselves. He empowers for mission.

3.
Motivated to Mission

Philippians 2:5–11; 2 Corinthians 5:17–21

At an unscheduled appearance before a Nationwide Bible Conference in Dallas, Texas, in March, 1971, Metropolitan Opera singer Jerome Hines told of his conversion to Christ. While writing an opera about the life of Jesus Christ, he found Christ as personal Savior. He then began what he called an apprenticeship for playing the life of Christ. He went to the places where he thought Christ would go; he did the things that he thought Christ would do. To the prisons, skid rows, and hospitals he went giving witness to Jesus Christ.

Jerome Hines was motivated to mission by the life of Christ.

The life of Christ serves as our strongest motivation to mission. When his life is examined, when his actions are analyzed, a Christian and his church receive overpowering motivation for mission.

In at least two places in the New Testament the apostle Paul centered motivation for Christian witness and mission in the life of Jesus Christ. His example serves as our strongest motivation.

When thoughts are turned to the incarnation and its meaning for our life, look at the incarnation from the standpoint of mission. Find in the life of Christ your motivation to mission.

Person

One of the most exalted statements of the person of Jesus Christ in the New Testament is found in Philippians 2:5–11. It is interesting to notice that this statement does not occur as a reasoned theological argument, but rather as a practical plea for Christian unity. Some interpreters feel that it is a fragment of an early Christian hymn.

To these fellow Christians Paul had expressed the desire that they serve together in unity and love. They were to be humble in their opinion of themselves and unselfish in their relations with others. To illustrate what he meant Paul appealed to the life of the Savior. He said, "Let this mind be in you, which was also in Christ Jesus" (Phil. 2:5). Or, as J. B. Phillips translated it, "Let Christ Jesus be your example as to what your attitude should be." Then he outlined the attitude of Christ Jesus in the verses that follow.

If this is to be the attitude of the Philippian Christians toward one another, it should also be the attitude of the church. As the church considers its mission, it should have the same attitude as the Lord of the church. From the example of Jesus the church received motivation to mission.

Humility. When Jesus accepted the incarnation, he accepted humility. Even though Jesus existed in the very form of God—he was one with God—he did not value that form so much that he selfishly grasped it to himself.

Instead, he emptied himself and took the form of a servant.

What humility that is! The very Son of God became a servant. The one who was present at the formation of the world became a servant in the world. Coming into the world as a man, he came as a servant. Upon limiting himself to the likeness of men, he humbled himself.

The church that was formed by faith in this same Jesus must serve with humility. As long as there is pride of place and the search for position, the church can hardly be a serving church.

To follow the example of Jesus, the church must humble itself enough to go where the people are and to get its hands dirty in ministry to people. Jesus became a man: he went where the people were. Jesus became a servant: he was willing to become involved in the lives of people.

No longer can a church erect a building, call a staff, structure a program, and expect people to come rushing to it. The church, instead, will need to humble itself enough to go to the people in their hurt, in their shame, and in their humiliation.

It may take humility for a church to conduct an outpatient clinic in a ghetto. It may take humility for a church to tutor children who have problems in school. It may take humility for a church to care for the children of working mothers. It may take humility for a church to send buses to impoverished areas to pick up children to bring to that church. These things cannot be done with haughty spirits and clean skirts. As Jesus was willing to humble himself enough to take upon himself our human plight, so must his followers be willing to humble themselves enough to serve human problems.

Servant. Jesus became a servant when he became a man. This gives to the church its most powerful figure for identification. The church must be a servant church.

To minister in this world, to carry out the mission of the church, the church must be a servant. As Jesus came into the world to minister rather than to be ministered unto, so does the church exist in the world to minister rather than to be ministered unto.

A well-known minister once asked a group of Chinese pastors what it was that impressed them most about Jesus. One elderly man replied, "His washing the disciple's feet." A servant action of Jesus, an enacted parable, the significance of which those Orientals could well understand, had drawn them to Christ.

Jesus made it very clear that he was a servant in the world. The servant role is the proper role for the church. Opportunities abound in every community for the church to be a servant. The climate of the times, rather than being a reason for retreat, can become a basis for expanding mission for the church that is willing to be a servant.

Obedience. Paul expressed in unforgettable language the spirit of obedience exhibited by Jesus. Notice: "And being found in human form he humbled himself and became obedient unto death, even death on a cross" (Phil. 2:8, RSV).

Jesus operated with a keen sense of obedience to the will of God. For him the will of God involved death—even death on the cross. But Jesus was obedient.

This same quality of obedience to the will of God is demanded by the church of God. As God reveals himself to the church and provides insight and opportunity for mission, that church must be obedient to the will of God.

Obedience to the will of God may demand radical departures. It could call for moving from study to simple acts of love; it could demand a departure from preaching to practical acts; it could suggest a change from socializing to social ministries.

Each church, as each individual, must search out the will of God for itself. What may be the mission opportunity for one church may not be for another church. Taking into consideration the constituents, the community, and the calling, each church can find God's will. After finding God's will in mission, obedience must follow.

There could also be times when obedience to the will of God would determine that an action be terminated. It often takes more courage to stop something than to start something. Yet in carrying out its mission the church may see that the need for a particular ministry no longer exists. Short-term mission projects have value. Also the need may have been met, or someone else may be meeting that need better than the church. Then that particular ministry could be terminated and another begun.

Exaltation. And what is the result of Jesus' loving action in becoming a man? The ultimate result is exaltation.

Paul stated that God has exalted him above all else. The name of Jesus is the name that brings awe and submission to all creatures. At some time every person would confess that Jesus Christ is Lord. Even the created universe would acknowledge his lordship.

Persons have the choice of voluntarily acknowledging the lordship of Jesus Christ or of having this confession wrung from them in judgment. Although all may not assent to the exalted state of Christ now, they will know it at some time.

And what of the servant church? If the church follows the example of Jesus in humility, servanthood, and obedience, will it be similarly exalted? The purpose of the church is not to exalt itself but to point to the exalted Christ. The greatest exaltation for the church is to see men confess Jesus Christ as Savior and accept him as Lord. When the church fulfills its mission, the result will be that Jesus is exalted.

J. Wallace Hamilton told of the time that Handel's *Messiah* was first played in England. It was played in a large hall in honor of Queen Victoria. It had already become the custom for people on the Continent to rise to their feet at the "Hallelujah Chorus," but everyone thought the Queen should remain seated because of her station. Yet when the great strains of the majestic music floated out: "And He shall reign for ever and for ever. He shall reign for ever and for ever," the Queen with fine insight got to her feet, lifted the crown from her head, and stood with bowed head with the rest. It was a prophecy of that day when every eye shall see and every knee shall bow and every tongue shall confess that Jesus Christ is Lord.[1]

"Jesus Christ is Lord" is the basic Christian confession of faith. It is probably the earliest Christian confession of faith. When the church is properly motivated to mission and people make that confession, it is exaltation enough for the church.

Plan

The reason that God became a man in Jesus Christ is expressed in a beautiful passage in 2 Corinthians 5:17–21. Jesus humbled himself to become an obedient servant for a reason. The reason was the reconciliation of man to God. Paul put it very succinctly:

"God was in Christ, reconciling the world unto himself" (2 Cor. 5:19).

Anyone who accepts this manifestation of God, Jesus Christ, as his personal Savior becomes a new person. God gives new life; he does not count man's previous sin against him. This has been forgiven through faith in Jesus Christ.

Then God has a plan. The plan is that those persons who have known Jesus Christ in faith are to be the agents of reconciliation themselves. They are commissioned by God to make this good news known to all people: people can be forgiven and have right standing with God. This is mission. And the motivation for it comes from Jesus Christ himself.

Reconciliation. The impulse to mission begins with the fact of reconciliation. It is not that God needs to be reconciled to man; it is that man needs to be reconciled to God. Man is the sinning one. His rebellion has created the barrier, the separateness between God and man. God has taken the initiative. He sent Jesus Christ into the world to reconcile persons to God.

The reconciliation is made possible through Jesus Christ. Jesus did not know sin. He was the perfect, sinless individual. Yet on the cross he bore the full brunt of the sin of the world. The one who had never experienced sin experienced the full results of sin in his own life.

Through faith in Jesus Christ we can be counted right with God. Righteousness does not come because a person has achieved it: it comes because in Jesus Christ God has considered him as righteous.

The good news of reconciliation sends the Christian into mission. Because he has experienced the grace of God in the forgiveness of sin, he wants others to have this same saving knowledge of God.

Reconciliation forms the foundation for mission. But without the person of Jesus Christ who came into the world to take our sins upon himself, there would be no reconciliation.

Reconcilers. Having experienced reconciliation, the believer becomes a reconciler. God has given to us a ministry or reconciliation.

We know what it is to be separated from others. The forces of separation are indeed powerful in our day. Separation is seen between races of people, between the sexes, between the educated and the uneducated, between the rich and the poor, between the young and the old, and between the believer and the unbeliever. The gospel of Jesus Christ cuts across all barriers that people have erected to bring all who will come to him to salvation. Things that once were separating factors are overlooked in salvation.

Jesus showed in his own life that the barriers can be jumped through faith in him. By his encounter with the Samaritan woman at the well he stepped across religious, racial, social, and sexual barriers to bring reconciliation to a woman and her God.

Finding our motivation in the life of Christ we are to be reconciling persons too. The Christian unifies rather than divides. The gospel of Christ shared in the grace of God leaps barriers to bring reconciliation.

The content of the reconciling message is that "God was in Christ reconciling the world unto himself." This is the source of unity between people who are otherwise divided. It is not simply a reconciliation between separated persons on the basis of a reconciliation with God. Sin separates; Christ unites.

Representatives. We, then, are to be the representatives of God in this world. "We are ambassadors for Christ," Paul proudly proclaimed.

A political ambassador is a representative of his country in a foreign land. He speaks for his country; he acts on the behalf of his country. A spiritual ambassador, an ambassador for Christ, is a representative of God on the earth. He speaks the reconciling message of peace and salvation through Jesus Christ; he lives for

God in his community.

You will notice that to be an ambassador for Christ you do not have to be appointed as a foreign missionary. You do not even have to be commissioned as a home missionary. As far as that goes, you do not have to be the official representative of your church. You do have to be a minister of reconciliation. You do have to be one who through both word and work proclaims that God was in Christ for the purpose of reconciling the world unto himself.

The message of reconciliation has been entrusted to us. The ministry of reconciliation has been given to us. By accepting Christ we become ambassadors for Christ, his representatives in our home community.

Mission is not always going; mission is sharing as you go, where you are. This is God's plan. This is your place in mission. The motivation for it is Jesus Christ himself.

The First Baptist Church in Jonesboro, Louisiana, is located in a rather small town in a basically rural parish [county] in North Louisiana. A large paper mill is located nearby. The economy of the parish is based on that paper mill and the forests that feed it. Jonesboro could probably be described as a typical parish-seat town in rural North Louisiana with all the problems as well as opportunities that description implies.

Motivated by a desire to live the life of Christ in their community the women of the church established "Benevolence House" in a borrowed building across the street from the church. Beginning with the collection and distribution of clothing to the victims of a devastating hurricane, the ministry has expanded to a continuous clothing program for needy persons. In addition to this the women supply food, household items, furniture, wheelchairs, and hospital beds to those who might need them. In Benevolence House itself there is also an apartment for overnight lodging and "His Place" for the young people. The men have helped with a "Toys for Tots" program during the Christmas season. From it has also developed a Headliner's Club and a course on "Abundant Living for House-wives" taught by the pastor. Their vision has not been limited to the home community. Through correspondence initiated by the Headliner's Club, they have collected materials and medical supplies for a mission hospital in the Philippine Islands.

When motivated to mission by the life of Christ, there is no end to what could be done by the people of a local church. The person and the plan coalesce. God has come to us in Jesus Christ. Because of what God has done in Jesus Christ, we are reconciled to him. As reconciled persons, we fit into the plan of God: we are to be ministers of reconciliation.

We can engage in no better exercise than to examine the person of Jesus Christ in order to accept his plan for us. Jesus is our strongest motivation to mission.

4.
The Meaning of Mission

Matthew 28:16–20; Mark 16:14–18; Luke 24:47–48; John 20:19–23; Acts 1:4–8

Theodore Wedel suggests that we could think of the church as a coast guard station on a dangerous coast. It has stood for centuries, and the tales of its rescue service are treasured by the successors of the founders. Stained-glass windows commemorate its heroes. In the course of time those who manned the rescue station have turned to expanding and beautifying the station itself. Architects vied with one another in building for them a dwelling place worthy of the cause which they serve. Honorary, though not active, members of the company of rescuers lent financial support. This station building, however, became in time such an absorbing activity that the rescue service itself was increasingly neglected, though traditional rescue drills and rituals were carefully preserved. The actual launching out into the ocean storm became a hireling vocation, or one left to a few volunteers.[1]

As tragic as it sounds, this parable may have happened to churches. The mission of the church may have been forgotten or relegated to only a few hardy souls willing to risk it. But this is not the purpose of Christ's church. The purpose of the church is mission.

The church was made for mission. As Christ lived the purpose of God in his coming into the world, the church is to live the life of Christ. Through his life, ministry, death, and resurrection, Jesus proclaimed the redemptive message of God through its mission.

What do we mean by mission? We often use the words "mission" and "missions," but what is the meaning of mission?

sions as commission. Acting on the commission of the risen Lord to all his followers, he began the modern thrust of mission activity.

Message

Those who proclaim the gospel to the unconverted everywhere have a message to share. Luke's version of the Great Commission, found in 24:44–49, indicated this.

Jesus had met with his disciples just prior to the ascension. He helped them in the interpretation of the Old Testament Scriptures, showing that they pointed to him. He showed again the centrality of the crucifixion and the resurrection. It was not just a mistake of history: it was in the plan of God.

Armed with this message, repentance and the forgiveness of sins should be preached to all nations by Jesus' followers today.

The mission message is the result of God's intention through the ages. It is his plan. Jesus came as the promised one of God. From the very beginning God had promised deliverance from sin. This deliverance came in the person of Jesus Christ. The Old Testament had its fulfillment in the babe born in Bethlehem.

The mission message has its basis in historical fact. The message is not some cunningly devised story or intricate scheme. It is based on the fact of the coming of Christ, his death on the cross for the sins of men, and his resurrection from the dead. The cross and resurrection taken together show the power of God in Jesus Christ over all the forces that oppose men: sin, self, Satan, and death.

The aim of the mission message is repentance and forgiveness. The two go together. Until one repents of his sin he cannot receive forgiveness.

The early disciples were the witness of what God had done through Christ. Their message would carry the stamp of authenticity because they had witnessed that of which they spoke.

Thus the aim of the mission message is to make believers. The proclamation of repentence and forgiveness in the name of Jesus

Christ results in people knowing Jesus Christ as Savior. One does not receive forgiveness from Christ without becoming a believer in Christ.

The scope of the mission message includes all the world. The message of redemption in Jesus Christ was not to be confined to Jerusalem; it was intended for all the world. Christ came to save all men from their sins. This message must be proclaimed to all nations. Jerusalem was just the starting point. Its destination was the world.

The promise of the mission message is the presence of power. Jesus advised the earliest disciples to stay in Jerusalem until they had received the promise of the Father. The promise was the power of the Holy Spirit activating their lives for God's mission in the world. They were not ready to proclaim the gospel to all nations until they received this power. The promise of the presence of God in the Holy Spirit both enables and empowers the mission message.

This is the same message that God had entrusted to present-day believers. Centered in God's great redemptive act in Jesus Christ, it is a message of hope, of deliverance, of forgiveness, and of life. It has not diminished in power nor in purpose in these intervening years. It is the mission of the church to proclaim the mission message.

Method

In the context of a question about Israel's national destiny, Jesus mentioned the method of missions. Found in Acts 1:6–8, this version of the Great Commission indicates something of the method to be used by the church in its mission.

When the disciples of Jesus were gathered for their farewell session with the Master, one asked him if the kingdom would be restored to Israel at that time. Since they were convinced that he was the Messiah, they had expected him to bring in the kingdom of God. In their minds the kingdom of God would be centered in

A classic definition of missions is that of Robert Hall Glover: "Christian missions is the proclamation of the gospel to the unconverted everywhere according to the command of Christ."

Missions, then, is the mission of the church. By living the life of Christ in the world, the church engages in the proclamation of the gospel to the unconverted.

The commission given by Christ to the church is found in several places in the New Testament. The most familiar source is probably Matthew 28:19-20. Luke records it in two spots: Luke 24:47-48 and Acts 1:8. John's version is located in John 20:19-23. Mark, too, has a reference to the Great Commission in Mark 16:14-18.

Probably one of the best ways to learn the meaning of mission is to refer to the commission for mission given by Jesus to the earliest disciples. Present-day disciples would do well to consider this their commission too. It is a total misunderstanding of the commission of Jesus to limit it only to those who heard it for the first time, or just to the original apostles, or just to the early church. This is our commission.

Commission

The passage of Scripture that we have identified as the Great Commission is found in Matthew 28:18-20.

The authority for the commission is centered in Jesus Christ. He said, "All authority in heaven and on earth has been given to me" (Matt. 28:18, RSV). The King James Version translates that "power." Authority is power.

The Christian does not get his authority for mission from the church, from the message of Christ, nor even from the Bible. The authority for mission comes from Jesus himself. He who has all authority for all things gives a foundation for mission by his authority.

"Make disciples" is the comprehensive task. The one who is a disciple of Christ, who knows Jesus Christ as his personal Savior, is to make disciples of others.

You will notice that this is to be the natural result of the disciple's life. "Go" could be translated "going" or "as you go." It is assumed that the followers of Christ will go. But as they go, their commission is to so live the life of Christ and to so proclaim the message of his redemption that disciples will be made.

Two components of the comprehensive mission of making disciples are mentioned: baptizing and teaching.

Baptism in the name of the Father, Son, and Holy Spirit is an act of obedience on the part of a believer. Having given himself by faith to Jesus Christ, then he identifies himself with the church, the body of Christ. Whenever a person accepts Christ, he accepts the full recognition of God's revelation of himself as Father, Son, and Holy Spirit.

The new disciple is to be taught. He is to be taught to observe all the things that Jesus has commanded. This takes a lifetime of learning. Through study, through worship, through prayer, and through communion with the living Lord, the things that Jesus taught are learned. We are to teach "all" that Jesus commanded. As much as we might like, we cannot pick and choose the portions of Jesus' teachings we will observe. To be obedient Christians we must learn and do all that he has commanded.

It seems an impossible mission. But to enable us, Jesus promised his presence. "I am with you always, to the close of the age" (Matt. 28:20, RSV), is his promise. There is nowhere that is outside the reach of God's active interest and protective love.

The meaning of the commission had been obscured in the life of the church. But in the latter part of the eighteenth century a Baptist preacher-cobbler named William Carey caught a vision of the meaning of the commission and its binding task. After prayer, preaching, and agitation, a missions society was formed and Carey was sent as its first missionary to India in 1792. This was the beginning of the modern missions movement. One man saw mis-

the kingdom of Israel. He had not restored the kingdom previously. Now, perhaps, he would do it in a dramatic fashion.

Jesus did not directly answer the question. Instead he corrected it. He shifted the emphasis from speculation about the future to their demonstration of the power of God in the present. He shifted their attention from national ambitions to world missions.

When the kingdom of God would come in its ultimate fulfillment was not for them, or us, to know. Their responsibility was for responsible witness during this life, on this earth, at this time.

It is assumed that the Christian mission will be empowered by God. He had already told the believers to stay in Jerusalem until they would be enveloped in, immersed by, the Spirit of God. This would empower them for the task at hand.

No mission method is effective unless it is accompanied by the power of God. Mission method is not manipulation; it is the manifestation of God's power in the fulfillment of God's purpose. The promise upon which mission method is built is the promise of the power of God filling the person.

Based upon the power of the Holy Spirit, mission method takes two directions.

The first is witness. This is how mission is carried out. It must be the personal witness to the power of God in Jesus Christ. We can witness of that which we have experienced. Without witness there is no mission.

One of the first converts in the mission ministry of W. B. Bagby in Rio de Janeiro, Brazil, was a young man named Francisco Florencio Soren. This young man was so thrilled by the consciousness of the miracle of God's grace that he walked many miles to the home of his parents to tell them of his wonderful discovery. His mother was furious that he had abandoned the Roman Catholic Church to become a "Protestant." Nevertheless, he continued his efforts to interpret the meaning of his experience to his parents. Finally, his mother told him: "Son, I do not want to hear any more about it. Do not talk to me unless you can talk about something other than your new religion."

On his next visit home he greeted his parents, then had nothing more to say. Finally, his mother could endure the silence no longer. She exclaimed: "Son, why are you not talking? Why are you so silent." The young man replied: "Mother, you forbade me to speak to you about Jesus Christ and his saving grace. If I cannot talk to you about Christ, what it means to be saved, and the assurance of salvation, then I have nothing to talk about." "If it means that much to you, Son," said his mother, "then tell me about it." And so he talked and talked until he led his parents to know Christ as Savior and Lord. He kept on talking to his friends about Christ. God called him to preach. He was for many years pastor of the First Baptist Church in Rio and was one of the spiritual giants in the pioneer days of Baptist work in the great country of Brazil.[2]

The second mission method is to carry the witness to the gospel in ever-widening circles, beginning where you are. Jesus told them to be witnesses of him, "in Jerusalem and in all Judea, and in Samaria, and unto the uttermost part of the earth." The gospel is worldwide. And we are to witness to Jesus Christ throughout the world.

But we begin our witness where we are. Jesus' followers were in Jerusalem at the time. You cannot wait until your Jerusalem is completely evangelized before you move in your witness to Judea, Samaria, and to points unknown. Witness begins right where you are. At the same time witness is extended into other areas. No limits are placed on the extent of the witness to Christ.

Neither are there time limits placed on the witness to Christ. Christians are to give witness to Christ until the very end.

Result

The meaning of mission is found in the result of mission activity. Mark's account of the Great Commission mentions result.

It must be recognized that the portion of Mark that includes the Great Commission, Mark 16:14–18, is not found in most of the best Greek manuscripts. Most authorities feel that the original work of Mark ended with verse 8. Through this passage we can see something of the result of mission, which is a part of its meaning.

The obvious result is that some people will believe on Jesus Christ as Savior and others will refuse to believe. In verse 16 Jesus said that those who believed, and on the basis of that belief, were baptized would be saved. It is not the baptism that saves but the belief. Those who do not believe would not be saved.

This result is at the heart of the meaning of mission. Because of Christian compassion and concern we are interested in people being saved. They cannot be saved unless the gospel is proclaimed to them. This is our task. We are not to force belief; we are to enable belief by our witness of Christ.

Another result is that those who believe on Christ will be empowered for effective witness to Christ. Many unusual manifestations are mentioned in this passage. At one time these may have been considered convincing signs of God's power. In our day they may not be the most convincing demonstrations of the power and presence of God. Suffice it to say, that when one believes in Jesus Christ he has a power in his life to enable him to meet the problems of life and to express a witness to God.

Were there no results, mission would have no meaning. In belief and power the meaning of mission comes into focus.

Purpose

The mission of Christian people is to live the life of Christ in the world. Jesus has come into our world; he lived, died, and rose from the grave. By this he revealed God to us and redeemed us from our sin. Now he is no longer physically present in the world. But his followers are. Our purpose, as his followers, is to continue his revelatory and redemptive purpose.

John clarified this in his rendering of the Great Commission. According to John, Jesus said to his disciples: "Peace be unto you: as my Father has sent me, even so send I you" (John 20:21). This implies that we are sent into the world for the very same task for which Christ was sent into the world. Jesus had a keen awareness that he was sent to do the will of God and not his own; so we are sent to follow Christ's will and not our own. Jesus was sent into the world to reveal God and to redeem men; we are sent to reveal him and to be a redeeming influence among men.

We do not have two missions: Jesus' mission and our mission. Our mission is Jesus' mission. We are to do his will and to reveal him. It is of Jesus that Christian witness is given.

Again reference is made to the empowering of God for the mission of God. Christian mission is not carried out in the power of the witness; it is carried out in the power of the Savior.

The redemptive message is the forgiveness of sin. Our purpose in living the mission of Christ is to bring men into a right relationship with God.

When a church or an individual decides to live the life of Christ, it may carry him in new directions and to new places. He will love rather than distrust the person of another ethnic group. He will covet for Christ the low-rent housing area or that apartment complex. He will devise ways of reaching the people in the ghetto. He will not be afraid of giving himself in personal ministries that tire, and discourage, and sometimes hurt. All of this Christ did.

The meaning of mission is found in the commission that Jesus Christ gave to his followers. It is our commission today. It is both individual and corporate. We are obedient to it both as individual believers and as churches. Neither the person nor the group can ignore it. It tells us what mission means.

5.

Ministry Is Mission

Matthew 25:31–46; Luke 5:17–26; Acts 3:1–10

The Walnut Street Baptist Church in Louisville, Kentucky, is an old (one hundred fifty years), large (five thousand two hundred members), church in a decaying, racially-mixed inner-city community. A strong evangelistic church, it is also interested in a ministry to the total needs of the people of its community. Wayne Dehoney, the pastor, has said, "Persons are at the center of the mission of the church." [1]

Consider some of the things this church has done in an attempt to minister. They have a help office in a walk-in storefront staffed by church volunteers to assist as a channeling service for people in need. Tutoring classes are conducted. A vigorous weekday activities program for all ages is conducted in an activities building. A thrift ship is operated by a group of retired women who repair usable clothing and bedding and sell it at reasonable rates to needy people. They have a staff minister of social work who involves a large number of people in personal aid and counseling. Activities of many kinds, including clubs, team and sports activities, Scouts, day camps, and retreats, are offered. In addition, they have become involved in the erection of Baptist Towers, a multistoried apartment building to provide low cost housing for the elderly and a neighborhood development corporation.

Ministry, simply speaking, is caring for others and sharing Christ and concern with them in meeting both their physical and spiritual needs. C. W. Brister has written in *Pastoral Care in the Church*: "The servant motif of ministry was established . . . as the

Bible's most characteristic way of viewing the people of God. The church, like her Lord, is to be in the world as one who serves." [2]

The Bible has many references that assure us that Christ had come into the world to minister. The shepherd figure, of course, is the most familiar. As a shepherd cared for his sheep, protected them, and guided them, Christ has given to us love, protection, and guidance. His church is to do the same in its world.

Ministry is not something added to the life of the church. It is essential to the very life of the church. Because a church is to be a community of loving people who care and share with others, it performs ministry.

For a church to be a ministering church it does not have to have special staff personnel or special facilities. It does have to have concern, compassion, and love. It must be willing to give of itself and its resources to meet human needs. The greatest resource any church has is people who care, people who are willing to get involved in the lives of others, people who will accept the ministering, servant role as their own.

Several passages of Scripture suggest themselves for study. Consider Matthew 25:31–46. It is one of the teachings of Jesus that directly relates to this subject. A ministering act of Jesus in Luke 5:17–26 is helpful to our understanding. And what about the early Christians? Look at Acts 3:1–10.

Appropriateness

A concern that some persons have about ministry involves its appropriateness. Is this really the kind of activity that a church and a Christian ought to do?

Jesus answered that question himself. In a parable which is also a prophetic picture of the judgment, Jesus graphically portrayed the importance of ministry to persons.

Even though the name Jesus is not mentioned in the parable, it is apparent that the "Son of man," which was one of Jesus' favorite titles for himself, refers to the Christ. All "nations" is understood as all the people of the world. The judgment of God does not omit any.

In this picture the people are separated as a Palestinian shepherd would divide his flock at night: the sheep on one side, the goats on another. The same standard of judgment is used for all—love as reflected in ministry. This is the type of love that grows out of a relationship with Christ. The shepherd can distinguish the sheep from the goats. God, who knows people's hearts, is able to distinguish the true believer from the mere professing believer.

As the Lord announces the judgment of each one of the blessed, those who had ministered in love, are sent to a place prepared for them from creation. The others are dispatched to a place prepared, not for men but for the devil and his associates. The distinction is obvious: blessedness for those who minister in Christ's name, punishment for those who refuse Christ's call.

Christ has identified himself with those in need. The indication is that those who were separated from him would have performed acts of ministry had they known that it was Christ in need. But Christ is identified with all who are in need. When ministering acts of love are performed even to those who seem undeserving, Christ is being served.

The ministering acts praised by the Lord were not spectacular acts. They were simple, practical things that anyone could do: giving food to the hungry, giving water to the thirsty, giving welcome to the stranger, giving comfort to the sick, and giving concern to the imprisoned. How many times have opportunities for ministry been refused because they did not seem spectacular enough? How many times have objections to ministry been made because the church did not have special buildings, special staffs, or special budgets for ministry? What the Lord commended were the simple things. Things that could be done without much money or material, just love and concern.

In the summer of 1971 a disastrous "rock festival" was convened at McCrea, Louisiana. It never did get off the ground. Thousands of young people were marooned in a rural area choked by dust, scorched by sun, and ridiculed by neighbors. As it was breaking up, the pastor of the Pineville Park Baptist Church, in Pineville, Louisiana, mentioned to his congregation that thousands of young people had gathered in an area in easy driving distance of the church and the church had done nothing to help them. That afternoon several of the men of the church drove to the area. They then went back to offer the young people "A Way Out." Taking cold water and sandwiches, they carried a bus to provide a way out for those who would go with them. Then they carried them to Pineville where they were given food, a place to bathe and clean up, and travel connections. This did not cost much money. But it did give some needed help to young people. And it gave some new attitudes and new incentives to some church people.

The ones who ministered to others had done it so unselfconsciously that they could not even remember it when the Lord indicated that they had served him. This was simply their response to human need. It was not done in a calculating manner, thinking that they would receive virtue by having done it. It was done as their normal reaction to a person in need.

Is it appropriate for a church to minister to others? The Master's own parable is eloquent answer to that question. Not only is it appropriate, it is expected. As Jesus gave himself to a ministry of loving compassion, so should his followers.

Approach

Having been convinced of the appropriateness of ministry the approach is often a problem. Look at an incident in the life of Jesus. He was teaching when four friends brought a crippled man to him. They took some extraordinary steps for their friend to meet Christ. The story is told in Luke 5:17–26. It gives us some ideas about the approach to ministry.

The purpose of ministry is to bring people to the presence of Jesus Christ. These four friends brought the man to Jesus but could not get to him because of the crowd of people. Being persistent people they went to the roof of the house, lifted the roofing material, and let their friend down on his pallet. The end result of all ministering activity is to bring another to the presence of Christ. It is not done in such a way that he will feel obligated. Nor is the proper approach to beat him over the head with the gospel. At some time one will ask, "Why have you done this?" And the answer will be: "Because we cared. Jesus Christ has come into our hearts and we care for you; he cares for you." It may be an oblique rather than a frontal approach, but it is a way to express the loving concern of Christ for persons.

This approach shows the possibilities of ministry. How many others would have been discouraged because of the crowd? A little ingenuity, a little thought will suggest possibilities for ministry that had never been unearthed before. The possibilities for ministry are all around us. We must be observant enough and interested enough to use them.

Some ministering acts will open new opportunities for other ministering acts. These men in this case were interested in ministry to their friend. When ordinary possibilities were closed, they looked to other ways. The Trinity Baptist Church in San Antonio, Texas, had become involved in ministry. Their mission churches provided out-patient clinics for Planned Parenthood, preschool programs, after-school tutoring programs, and study halls. Through a Benevolence House the church had provided food, clothing, and supplies to people through several local organizations. They operate Alpha House, a ministry for women alcoholics. Then when the County Children's Home had to be closed for lack of funds they looked to the Trinity Baptist Church which assumed this responsibility.[3] Each ministering possibility suggested new possibilities. The possibilities are all around. Imagination, ingenuity, and incentive will bring them to light.

The performance of ministry is well illustrated by the loving act of these friends. They had given priority to the task of helping their paralytic friend. Ministry must be a priority item. It is not done by accident.

And it may take patience. People with lesser determination would have been discouraged long before these men were. In any ministering activity it will be easy to become discouraged. At times the barriers may seem to be more numerous than the blessings.

Persistence pays off. These men were so persistent that their friend reached his goal: he was brought to the presence of the healing Christ. More than one attempt may have to be made before the ministering project is carried to completion. Persistence may be a necessary virtue in the approach to ministry.

The promises of ministry are always present in any approach to ministry. Christ promised healing to those who came to him. But in the process this man received more than healing—he also received the forgiveness of his sin.

When the man suddenly appeared before Jesus after having been lowered through the roof, Jesus said, "Man, your sins are forgiven you" (Luke 5:20, RSV). The religious leaders who were present questioned this. By forgiving sins Jesus was taking the prerogative of God. Only God could forgive sin.

Knowing their problem, Jesus asked them if it were easier to say to the man that his sins were forgiven or to tell him to rise and walk. Obviously, it would be easier to *say* that sins were forgiven. There could be no way of checking this. But if Jesus told the man to rise and walk they could easily determine whether he had done it. Jesus had to prove the spiritual by the physical.

They had thought that sins and suffering were related. The man could be cured only if he were forgiven. They could not see the forgiveness of sin but they could see the healing of his paralysis.

So Jesus did what they would have considered to be the hardest thing: He healed the man. He proved his spiritual power by a physical act.

There are times when the only way we can prove our spiritual power is through physical acts of ministry. The promises of God are valid. There is healing with the Savior. Our ministry helps others to know this healing, both in the physical and in the spiritual realms. When we take the approach of these four friends of the paralytic, others will be blessed through the power of the Christ in their lives.

Answer

Do Christian people have an answer to human need? Most assuredly so. Consider an incident in the life of the early Christians as recorded in Acts 3:1–10.

How long after the Pentecostal experience this occurred we do not know. At this time the disciples of Christ were also observing the Hebrew forms of worship. On the way to the Temple at the morning hour of prayer Peter and John met a lame man who was brought every day to the Temple area to beg. When he asked for their aid, they requested that he look at them. Apparently he was not in the habit of looking at his benefactors. Then Peter said a memorable word to him: "I have no money at all, but I will give you what I have: in the name of Jesus Christ of Nazareth I order you to walk!" (Acts 3:6, TEV).[4] Then he helped him to stand and he was able to walk!

There were many questions that Peter and John could not answer that morning. They could not answer the question of the reason for the man's lameness, the origin of illness, nor the cause for his poverty. But they could answer the call for help. And they gave that answer in the power of Jesus Christ.

Many questions may present themselves that we cannot answer. We cannot answer the questions concerning the origin of suffering, nor how people get caught in the cycle of poverty, or why some suffer and others do not. But we can come with the answer of the compassionate Christ to minister to the needs of these people. We can state the answer that we do have.

Some questions that we often consider important questions are shown to be irrelevant questions by the action of Peter and John. For instance, they did not ask if the man deserved to be healed. Neither did they ask whether he would appreciate their action in ministering to him. Perhaps we have spent too much time seeking an answer to the irrelevant questions to consider the really relevant questions.

The relevant question is whether we have compassionate concern and a willingness to minister. When we answer that question, then we can get on with the job of ministering.

As we give the Christian answer to man's need by ministering in the name of Jesus Christ, we will dwell on what we *do* have, not on what we *do not* have. Many people have not acted because of what they do not have. Peter was aware of what they did not have, they did not have silver and gold to offer him, but they did have something far greater. And Peter was aware of that too. That is what they gave the man. Think of all the ministry in Christ's name that could be performed if we would adopt this positive approach rather than the negative approach we so often use.

All ministry must be done in the spirit and in the power of Christ. Peter commanded the man "in the name of Jesus of Nazareth." "In the name of" means "in the power of" or "by the authority of." God has given Christians the power to minister. This is what lifts Christian ministry above humanitarianism: it is done in the spirit and in the power of Jesus Christ.

Nothing can take the place of this power and motivation for ministry. In commenting on this passage a pope once said, "We do not now have to say, 'silver and gold have I none . . .'" And someone replied: "Neither can you say, 'rise up and walk!'" Working in the power of the risen Lord, ways can be found to minister even if there is not much money.

When the church starts examining its mission, ministry stands out as an integral part. Rather than being an optional alternative in Christian service it is an absolute essential. Catching the mood of Christ's actions, the meaning of his teaching, and the method of the early Christian's concern we can have ministering churches too. That is our mission.

6.
Witnessing Is Mission
Luke 10:1–16; 8:26–39; Acts 1:8; Colossians 4:5–6

The late Samuel M. Shoemaker once wrote: "The test of a man's conversion is whether he has enough Christianity to get it over to other people." After that statement, he related that at one time he could not do that. When he was seventeen years of age, he began lay reading in a small Episcopalian congregation. Two or three men in the group met tragic experiences because what he had given them was so general there was no conversion in it. He could not get it across. There followed a recurrent pattern of failure—at those services and working in army camps during World War I. Individuals were seeking spiritual help, but he could not give it to them. Then he went to China to teach in a school in Peking. Again men were seeking. He indicated that he would have failed them too, but he met a man in China who challenged him as to whether he had ever made a full commitment of his life to Jesus Christ. And he held him to it until he did. The very next day a Chinese businessman made his Christian decision with him. Shoemaker suggested: "Test yourself by this: Can I get across to other people what I believe about Jesus Christ? If not, what real good am I to them, and what real good am I to Him?" [1]

We call the process of getting across what you believe and what you have experienced with Jesus Christ witnessing. D. T. Niles once defined Christian witness very well as "one beggar telling another beggar where to find bread."

Witnessing is mission. As the church lives out the life of Jesus Christ in the world, it must express to the world that Jesus Christ is both the secret and the source of its life. This is done by individuals witnessing for Christ.

A witness shares an experience. He tells another person what he has experienced with Jesus Christ. In a courtroom a witness tells only what he personally knows about the incident under question. He is not allowed to tell what he thinks, what another has seen, or what another has experienced. He must speak out of his own knowledge and experience. Ralph W. Neighbour, Jr., in a booklet entitled *Witness, Take the Stand!* has well said, "I am never witnessing until I am: (1) Speaking to a lost person (2) about my personal knowledge (3) of the Lord Jesus Christ." [2]

Witnessing is at the very heart of the mission of the church. All that a church does points to Jesus Christ. Christ is at the very center of its existence; he is the cause of its existence. The people who have met Jesus Christ as Savior and have been called into being by his spirit for the purpose of fellowship, mission, and proclamation, must be active witnesses of the grace of God.

From several New Testament passages it is evident that witnessing is mission, and that this is the responsibility of the Christian people who form the church.

Authorization

The authorization for witnessing is given by Jesus himself. This is clearly stated in an incident in the life of Jesus when he sent out seventy persons on a witnessing mission. It is found in Luke 10:-1–16.

Earlier (Luke 9:16) he had sent the twelve, the apostles, on a similar mission. This time, however, he chose seventy persons to witness of him in the area.

The number of people chosen is significant. Obviously, because of this number, these were not only the persons whom we usually designate the disciples, or the apostles. These were people who did not accompany Jesus at all times. They did know him; they could witness of him. Seventy is the same number that Moses chose to help in the task of leading and directing the people in the wilderness (Num. 11); it was also the number in the Sanhedrin, the supreme council of the Jews.

The number of nations in the world was considered to be seventy. This might have the most significance. Luke projects a universalist vision; the gospel is for all people. The number of people sent out to witness may speak of the time when the gospel is known by all people in all the world. Indeed, the gospel knows no boundaries. The witness of Christ is to be shared with all the people of the world.

Jesus commissioned them to go in his name. By pairs they went into the areas where he was later to go himself. As he sent them he reminded them that they were laborers in the harvest for God. The harvest was plentiful; all around are persons who need to experience the grace of God. The problem is the shortage of laborers. Always there has been a shortage of people willing to witness.

As Christians, we are to pray that there will be more witnesses. But it cannot stop there. We cannot pray for witnesses without being willing to be witnesses.

And we cannot assume that everyone will gladly hear the witness and positively respond to it. Jesus warned them that he was sending them "as lambs among wolves" (Luke 10:3). Even though the possibility of rejection becomes such a frightening thing to some that they never witness, it is not to be a deterent. Neither rejection nor ridicule removes the responsibility for witness.

Something of the urgency of the witness is conveyed by Jesus. They were not to carry heavy baggage; they were not to spend time in long greetings; they were not to stay at places where they were not welcome; they were not to complain of the accommodation. They were sent with one purpose in mind: the announcement of the salvation of God in Jesus Christ. They could not be sidetracked by irrelevant details. The urgency of the message superseded the details with which they might be concerned.

The announcement is one of Christ. They were to heal the sick in Christ's name and to proclaim, "The kingdom of God has come near to you" (Luke 10:9, RSV). The kingdom of God centers in Jesus Christ. When one has accepted Christ by faith he has become a citizen of God's kingdom.

The announcement of the Christian witness is always Christ. It may be easier to talk about the church, or the preacher, or the program. For it to be witness, it must be the announcement of Christ.

Those who hear have a responsibility. To have heard the witness of Christ is to be responsible for a response to Christ. Jesus cited places (vv. 13–15) which carried a heavier responsibility because they had not responded to the message of Christ.

The authorization for witness is summarized in Jesus' departing statement to them: "He who hears you hears me, and he who rejects you rejects me, and he who rejects me rejects him who sent me" (Luke 10:16, RSV). It is on the authority of Jesus himself that the Christian witness bears his witness. To reject the witness of Christ is to reject Christ.

Aim

The aim of Christ is that all believers serve as witnesses to him. This he enunciated just before the ascension. As recorded in Acts 1:8 Jesus said, "And you shall be my witnesses in Jerusalem and in all Judea and Samaria and to the end of the earth" (RSV).

To be a witness is not an option with the Christian. Jesus said, "You *shall* be my witnesses." There is no choice about *whether* a Christian will be a witness. The only choice concerns *what kind* of witness he will be.

In the seventeenth century Thomas Hobson rented horses at Cambridge, England. He had a rule that any person who rented a horse must take the one standing nearest the stable door. No matter what station in life the customer held, nor how much he might argue or wheedle, Hobson stuck to his rule. Soon "Hobson's choice," which was really no choice at all, became a familiar statement and passed into colloquial usage.

Christians are confronted with "Hobson's choice" about witnessing. The only choice we have is the kind of witness we will be.

The content of the Christian witness is again emphasized. "My witnesses," is how Jesus described it. We find it easy to talk about various things. The Christian witness is to talk about Christ. Salvation has come because Jesus Christ has been accepted as Lord and Savior.

The most authentic witness is the personal testimony. An argument may be refuted. Logic may be imperfect. A personal experience cannot be lightly dismissed. This much the individual certainly knows; this was his own experience. Notice how often in the New Testament one person brought another to Jesus. He did it because he had met Christ himself and had found salvation in him. It began with Andrew who "first found his brother Simon, and said to him, 'We have found the Messiah' " (John 1:46, RSV). And from there it has continued to the present. One person introduces another person to Christ. That is the content of the Christian witness: Jesus Christ.

Consider the comprehensiveness of the witness. Christian witness begins right where the individual is and continues in ever-widening circles. From Jerusalem, where they then were, to Judea, to Samaria, and even to the end of the world, the Christian witness was to spread.

Often this is used as a basis for the discussion of local, state, home, and foreign missions. That might be valid. But the significant thing is that mission, Christian witness, begins where you are. Then it moves out in ever-widening circles to cover the world. Witnessing cannot be limited. Missions know no boundaries. If one is to engage in overseas witnessing, he first should have engaged in local witnessing. Concern for people in another locality should be rooted in a concern for those in the present locality. It is primarily a matter of widening the focus of the witness.

It is Christ's aim that all Christians become active Christian witnesses. God works through people. As one person tells another person about Christ they are brought to him in faith.

In a poem by George Eliot the truth of the importance of the person in God's work is stressed. In answer to the disdain of the work of making the violin by an artist the poet has Antonio Stradivari, the maker of the now priceless Stradivarius violins, answer:

> I say not God Himself can make man's best
> Without best men to help Him . . . 'Tis God gives skill,
> But not without men's hands; He could not make
> Antonio Stradivari's violins
> Without Antonio.

And God cannot give witness to other people of his saving acts through Jesus Christ without persons willing to proclaim it.

Answer

A compelling reason that the Christian is a witness of Christ is that he might be able to give an answer for his faith. What is it that makes a Christian different? What is it that causes him to love? What is it that has awakened concern for others? What is it that causes him to share his faith, his experience with Christ? The answer is that he has found Christ. In his experience with Christ he has an answer for his life.

Paul expressed this in two verses in Colossians. He wrote, "Conduct yourselves wisely toward outsiders, making the most of the time. Let your speech always be gracious, seasoned with salt, so that you may know how you ought to answer every one" (Col. 4:5–6, RSV).

The answer of the Christian is seen in the kind of life that he lives. Paul referred to those who did not know the Savior as "outsiders." To them the believer shows a life that has a distinctive difference to it: the difference that is marked by God's love. That is itself a witness.

A man who was found unconscious on the street was once brought to a private hospital for care. Upon regaining consciousness he began to abuse everyone who came to his room to minister to him. Finally only one nurse would go near the difficult patient. She alone endured the foul language, bathed him, changed the linens, and brought his meals.

On a Friday, the nurse came early and told the man that she would be leaving early to go to a Baptist student retreat and that she would miss taking care of him over the weekend. Then the man told her that he would not be there when she returned. He was being taken to a charity hospital.

"Since this is good-bye," he said, "will you explain to me why you continued to take care of me, despite my behavior and bad language, when no one else bothered with me?" "I believe that God loves you," she responded, "and he may want to love you through me." The patient reached up and pulled two dollars from under his pillow and said, "Here, please take this; it is all I have. Buy a box of candy for the students at the retreat; it is a gift that love sends, for through you I have seen love for the first time."

We are to seek every opportunity for giving our Christian witness. Paul counseled about "redeeming the time" (KJV) or "making the most of the time" (RSV) or "making good use of every opportunity you have" (TEV). Opportunities often pass unaccepted. When an opportunity to witness to a particular person or in a specific manner presents itself, it should be accepted. It may not come again. All the opportunities for witness must be seized as they come.

The Christian answer should be gracious. The integrity of the person should not be violated. Few people are bulldozed into the kingdom of God. The exact manner in which the witness is given may vary between individuals. In witnessing a memorized speech is not as important anyhow as a shared experience. With winsomeness and genuine interest the Christian gives his answer: Christ makes the difference in the life.

Appointment

Each of us has been given an appointment to witness by Jesus. Since we have experienced salvation by the grace of God, we are appointed witnesses of the great grace.

Turn to one of the personal encounters of Jesus to verify this appointment. In Luke 8:26–39 the intriguing story of the healing of the Gadarene demoniac is recorded.

This unfortunate man who was known as Legion, for it seemed that a legion of demons lived in him, lived in the cemetery. He could not be restrained; he removed his clothes; he broke the ropes and chains that bound him. Recognizing Jesus he asked him not to torment him. Jesus cleansed the man. The demons were cast out and directed to a herd of pigs who plunged over a cliff to their death. The herdsman rushed into the nearby town to tell the news.

When the people returned they found a most amazing thing. Legion was sitting, clothed and in his right mind, with Jesus. The power of God in Jesus Christ had completely transformed this man. So frightened were the people that they asked Jesus to leave.

The man from whom the demons had been cast wanted to go along with Jesus. Think how great this would have been. He could have accompanied the Master in his preaching mission. He could give a personal testimony of what the grace of God had done for him. "From Demoniac to Disciple" would have been a fine Thursday night topic.

But notice the appointment Jesus gave to him: "Go back home and tell what God has done for you" (Luke 8:39, TEV). He was not to go to far distant places to give his witness. He was to return to his home, to the place where he was best known, to witness. From his personal experience to the people who knew him best he could tell of the work of God in changing a life.

Where is our appointment for witness? Right where we are. We may consider it more glamorous, and a lot easier, to go to places where people do not know us. But if we are unable to witness where we are we will never be able to witness effectively at other places.

To be a witness where you are does not lessen the commitment to mission in other places. Instead, it gives substance to it. It is itself a witness to the fact that you are serious about witness, that the Christian mission has been accepted as your mission.

Having accepted the appointment to witness where you are then you can begin your witnessing efforts. It may mean sharing your Christian experience with a friend. It may mean inviting a few friends over for coffee and then using that opportunity to discuss Christ and his meaning for our lives. It may mean making scheduled visits to witness to unbelievers. It may mean changing your approach to life in order that the strength of the words might be matched by the winsomeness of the personality. It may mean becoming a better wife and mother so that your family will know that you mean it when you say that Christ can change the life for better.

Do not be disappointed if you cannot serve in exciting and glamorous places. The appointment given to us by Christ is to witness where we are.

As the overall mission of the church is examined, witnessing is seen to be an integral ingredient. No matter where the gospel is presented, or what form the presentation has taken, someone must put it in words: it is Jesus Christ who gives to us new life. Christian concern eventuates into Christian witness.

7.
Fellowship Is Mission

John 13:31–35; 15:12–17; 2 Corinthians 8:1–7; Philippians 4:14–19; 1 John 1:1–7

From a chance encounter at a grocery store in Dallas, Texas, photographer Bill Hammett introduced a hippie-type drug user known only as Eddie to Christ. After their first meeting when the door to the store was blocked by a group of rough talking, long-haired, dirtily dressed young people, Eddie followed the photographer to his car where a Christian witness was given during the course of their conversation. Hammett ended that visit with the promise, "When you decide you really want to be helped, I will help you."

A few days later the pastor of the Shiloh Terrace Baptist Church in Dallas, who later told the story in the *Baptist Standard*, received a letter from Eddie asking him to contact Bill Hammett; Eddie wanted to see him but did not know how to reach him. A week later he made his decision to accept Christ as Savior.

With the acceptance of Christ as Savior he also gave up drugs, surrendered himself to a narcotics agent, and received withdrawal treatment in a state hospital. An uncle, who was a Baptist deacon, took him into his family and his church. Eddie went back to high school and graduated. Then a week after graduation he was in a fatal automobile accident.

In commenting upon the Christian fellowship that he had discovered, Eddie said: "You Christians don't realize what you've got. The kind of friends and fellowship I had before are no match for this!" [1]

The fellowship of Christians is an integral part of the mission of the church. As the church lives the life of Christ in the world, it shows a fellowship that is uniquely its own. This fellowship is a feature that attracts to Christ and witnesses of the Christian experience.

The word that we translate "fellowship" is an important New Testament word that is used in a variety of ways. It can express participation, or sharing, or communion, or the close spiritual relationship between the believer and Christ or the believer and other believers. But basic to the word is the sense of a unique community of belief and faith. It is a life that is lived in community, taking into consideration our commitment to Christ and our response to one another.

The church does not *have* a fellowship as much as it is a fellowship. In speaking of the church as an institution Elton Trueblood said in *The Incendiary Fellowship*, "we must have more than institutions; we must have genuine communities." Some have found a distinction between society and a community. A society exists because of a common purpose. A community shares a common life. The Christian church must be a community. The people of the church have had a common experience of new life in Jesus Christ; they then share that common life. The fellowship that is central to Christian community is part of the mission of the church.

Several aspects of the unique fellowship of Christians are apparent from a study of selected passages of Scripture.

Attitude

Jesus identified one distinguishing attribute for the Christian: love. The attitude of love that the believer has toward God and toward other Christians forms the basis for fellowship.

In John 13:31–35 Jesus discussed that quality of life with the disciples.

It was the night of the Last Supper. Judas had just left the apostolic group. When he left, Jesus commented that now he would be glorified and that God would be glorified by him. John's Gospel used "glorify" to describe the events of the death, burial, and resurrection of Jesus. By this redemptive event glory would come to God. But you will notice that glory will both come from God and return to God. This was a divine act from beginning to end.

Jesus told them that he would be departing and that they could not come with him. Then he gave them a new commandment.

The new commandment was "that you love one another; even as I have loved you, that you also love one another" (John 13:34, RSV). But immediately we stop short. This is not a new commandment. The commandment to love was an old commandment. But into this new commandment Jesus breathed new life.

T. B. Maston in *Biblical Ethics* has pointed out several ways that it is a new commandment. It is new in its source. The source is from Jesus himself. In its motive it is new. Jesus said, "as I have loved you." Our response to Christ is to love him. If we love him, we will keep his commandments. His primary commandment is to love. This commandment is new in its nature. It sets forth a spirit, an attitude, that is to permeate the Christian community. It is not a legalism, but an obedience that evolves from a relationship. It is new in its dimensions. There is a peculiar and distinctive love for other Christians. In its depth it is new. Believers are to love one another as Jesus loved them. That would involve service and sacrifice. The results are new. Men would know the Christians by the quality of their love.[2]

This attitude of love is to be the distinguishing mark of Christians. Early in the Christian experience the heathens remarked, "See how the Christians love one another."

Relationship

The attitude of love defines the relationship that Christians have to one another. John 15:12–17 records the continuation of a long discussion between Jesus and his earliest followers. The commandment to love one another is repeated in verses 12 and 17.

William Barclay has remarked: "We are sent out into the world to love one another. Sometimes we live as if we were sent into the world to compete with one another, or to dispute with one another, or even to quarrel with one another. But the Christian is sent into the world to live in such a way that he shows what is meant by loving his fellow man." [3]

Something of the extent of love is shown in verse 13 when Jesus said, "Greater love has no man than this, that a man lay down his life for his friends" (RSV). This identifies the extent of Jesus' love for us; he was willing to give his life for us. In response to this, we maintain our relationship to him by love and to other Christians by love.

We can be called the friends of Jesus. One difference between a friend and a servant is that a servant would not necessarily know what the master was doing. But a friend would. Jesus has shown the greater love in laying down his life for us, his friends. And he has also demonstrated that we are friends and not servants by taking us into his counsel. He has revealed to his followers what he has received from the father.

And now what should be the response of the friends of Jesus? Obedience. Having been chosen by Christ rather than initially choosing Christ, his followers are to produce fruit in their lives. The fruit of the Christian is a Christlike life.

Seeking to live the Christlike life, the Christian can make his deepest requests to God, the Father, through the name of Christ and his prayer will be heard.

Neither the individual Christian nor the church can live the life of Christ in the world without love. Love forms the relationship with others. Seeking to produce a Christlike life, Christians also show the love of Christ in fellowship.

It is the love of Christ and the strength of Christian fellowship that would prompt people to help others in their personal development by teaching sewing, giving personal grooming information, guiding in nutrition and cooking, and giving child-care help. From the fellowship of Christians comes the impetus to teach others to read, to tutor children, and to teach English to those who do not speak it. The relationship of love to others determines that the disadvantaged and the poor be given some aid in their difficulty.

Fellowship cannot be divorced from mission action. The strength of Christian fellowship expressed in the relationship of love decides the question.

Communion

The communion that we have with God and with one another is the aspect of fellowship that is emphasized in 1 John 1:1–7. Four times in these verses the word "fellowship" is used according to the Revised Standard Version.

Through this epistle John is showing that Jesus was the real Christ who came into the world to bring God's revelation and redemption. Against those who thought and taught that Jesus was just something less than God or something more than man, John made it explicit that they had known him, seen him, and touched him.

This Christ has now been proclaimed that those who know him might have fellowship with other Christians. And this fellowship is with both God, the Father, and Jesus Christ, the Son.

Knowing Jesus Christ in salvation is like walking from the darkness to the light. God is light. And his people live in the light of his revelation. All who walk in the light of God's love have fellowship with one another.

The Christian life cannot be lived in isolation. With the Christian faith there is a communion with God and with one another. The person who would try to be a Christian in isolation from other Christians denies himself the communion that he can have with them. Such a person also denies himself the sense of community that is the fellowship of the church.

It is the communion that we have with God and with one another that establishes mission. From communion with God comes the impulse to share. From communion with other Christians comes the ingredients of sharing with others. Whether it is the sharing of a word of witness, a message of hope, a bit of encouragement, a piece of furniture, an article of clothing, a bite to eat, or an opportunity for expression, it is shared from the Christian fellowship in a spirit of love.

This is the reason that mission cannot be conducted in isolation from worship. Through worship we have communion with God. Through worship we come together as a Christian community. From one another we derive information, inspiration, and strength for our Christian mission. Apart from the worship of God and the witness of the word much mission action could degenerate into mere humanitarianism. It is the communion that we have with God and with one another that keeps mission as mission. Fellowship provides perspective.

Sharing

Fellowship involves sharing. As Christians, we share faith, but we also share things. This is illustrated in 2 Corinthians 8:1–8.

Paul had been interested in taking a collection for the relief of the suffering Christians in Jerusalem. He was gathering this gift from the Gentile churches in order to show their unity in the faith and to show the Christian concern that these Christians had for the Jewish Christians. It was a tremendous demonstration of Christian fellowship. Christians of other lands, of other racial and national groups, would share what they had with Christians in need.

Illustrative of the depth of fellowship displayed were the Macedonian churches. Paul used their example to prod the Corinthian church, too. The Macedonian Christians were not wealthy. In fact, they gave far beyond their means in contributing to this gift. Both their joy in their giving and their poverty from which they gave combined to make their gift a wealth of liberality.

Paul shared the secret of this kind of liberal sharing. It comes from being willing to first give oneself to the Lord (2 Cor. 8:5). When a Christian or a church has first committed himself to the Lord, then he will be willing to share in helping to meet the needs of others.

This is forcefully demonstrated in the life of the early church. In Acts 4:32–37 the story is told of the response of these Christians to the needs of others. So concerned were they about the other believers that they did not consider their own things their own. They willingly sold their possessions to help meet the needs of others. The Macedonians had learned their secret of sharing. It begins with giving oneself to the Lord. Then sharing results as the response of the concerned Christian.

This same kind of sharing between Christians and between churches can be practiced today.

In the little Methodist Chapel in the English village of Watlington there is an unusual collection of hymnbooks. Outwardly they resemble any other Methodist hymnbooks, but on the inside cover each bears this unique inscription: "Presented to the Watlington Methodist Church by the Chinese Methodist Churches of Hong Kong, 1953." This is the story as related by Leonard Griffith.

The Rev. Arthur Bray came to Watlington in 1952 after a distinguished missionary career of twenty-five years in China. He had returned to England to spend his few years before retirement in whatever small rural community needed him. He found a dismal situation in Watlington: a church building dreadfully dilapidated, the plaster crumbling off the walls, and the roof badly in need of repair. He tried to get the people to do something about it, but with no result. There were too few of them; they had no money; even the Methodist Conference could promise no help.

One day, after a season of prayer, Arthur Bray wrote to some sympathetic friends in Hong Kong, sharing his problem with them and asking if they would care to assist privately. Before leaving the East he had helped them to build a church building and he knew that the morale of Christian people rises when they have a house of worship of which they could be proud. These good friends not only sympathized. Like the Macedonians in Paul's letter, they welcomed the privilege of demonstrating their gratitude to the parent church which had given them birth and had done so much for them. They canvassed the entire Chinese Methodist community in Hong Kong and collected sufficient funds to finance the repair and redecoration of the Watlington chapel as well as the provision of those hymnbooks containing their memorable inscription.[4]

Participation

By Christian fellowship we participate in the work that others do. Paul expressed this beautifully in Philippians 4:14–19.

The word that is in the King James Version translated "communicate" and in the Revised Standard Version translated "share" in verse 14 and "entered into partnership" in verse 15 is a derivative of the word that is usually translated "fellowship." It was a part of the fellowship that these Philippian Christians shared with Paul that they could participate in his mission.

Paul indicated that this was a fellowship that he had only with this church. Others had not given him financial help. But this church had helped him more than once. He also made it clear (v. 17) that he did not seek the gift that they had sent him. He did feel that by the gift they would participate in his ministry. Whatever credit he received for what he did would be shared with them.

Giving never makes the giver poorer. God supplies all the needs out of the abundance of his riches in Christ Jesus. We participate in the life and ministry of others by our Christian fellowship that shares with others in their mission.

This is the very reason that we do not support missionaries; we are missionary. If we simply supported missions and missionaries, we would just send them money from time to time. If we are missionary, then we will participate with them in the mission work that they do wherever they are.

This also lifts financial involvement in missions from the level of mere giving to mission participation. We do not simply give gifts; we give ourselves. And it is an outgrowth of the Christian fellowship.

Fellowship is mission. The Christian fellowship is such a strong and a unique relationship of love that it both expresses and is part of our Christian life. Mission would fall flat without fellowship. Fellowship is the source of mission.

8.
Using Various Gifts in Mission

Luke 13:6–9; 1 Corinthians 12:4–31; 2 Corinthians 4:7; Ephesians 4:11–16; 5:22–27

What kind of persons does God use in mission? The truth is that God uses all kinds of persons.

God can use the ordinary people. Look at the first twelve disciples. They were certainly ordinary folks! Paul reminded the Corinthian Christians, "Now remember what you were, brothers, when God called you. Few of you were wise, or powerful, or of high social status, from the human point of view" (1 Cor. 1:26, TEV).

God can use the well educated. Paul was certainly well educated. The contribution of men like E. Y. Mullins and John A. Broadus to both the academic and practical life of Baptists is almost beyond computation.

But God can also use the ill educated. John Bunyan, the tinker, William Carey, the shoemaker, and William Booth, the pawnbroker's assistant, all lacked formal education; but each turned innumerable people to God and each remains unforgotten in the story of Christian faith.

God can use the disfigured. George Whitefield, the famous evangelistic contemporary of the Wesleys, was so cross-eyed that when he made the mistake of saying, "That man. That man I am looking at now," two men always came under conviction.[1]

God can use the person with one talent. It is said that Philip Bliss had the single talent of versification. Even though not considered to be a poet, he wrote hymns that pointed people to the Savior for many years.

God can use the obscure. No one knows the name of the

preacher who urged Charles Haddon Spurgeon to "look and live."

God can use all sorts of persons in mission. The only real qualification is that the person must be willing to be used.

Any given gathering of Christians will include people with varying talents, gifts, and abilities. There will be people who can do some things well while they cannot do other things well at all. But each person is valuable in his own right. His particular ability can well be used by Christ and his church.

This is a significant reminder for mission. Mission can be carried on through various gifts. This is a practical reminder. Each person can find a place of service in which his own gift can be used. But it is also a scriptural reminder. At several places in the Bible recognition is given of this fact. Consider a few of them and their implications for the mission of the church.

Person

In 2 Corinthians Paul felt compelled to defend his apostleship. He felt that his ministry had been given to him by God. By preaching Jesus Christ he had been an instrument of God's service. The same God who had commanded the light to shine out of the darkness in creation had been dispelling the darkness from human lives through regeneration.

Then he made a tremendous statement in 2 Corinthians 4:7 when he said, "But we have this treasure in earthen vessels, to show that the transcendent power belongs to God and not to us" (RSV).

The treasure, of course, is a reference to the treasure of the redemptive message of God. Of all the valuable things in this earth, the most valuable is the message of salvation through faith in Jesus Christ.

This great treasure, however, is contained in earthen vessels. Who would ever expect to find a collection of rare gems in an old clay pot? And who would expect to find the treasure of God's redemptive message of love entrusted to fallible, weak, persons?

But this is how God has chosen to work. He has entrusted his message to persons.

There is a reason why God entrusted his message to persons: to show that the power of God belongs to him and not to us. By working through persons to present his message to other persons, it is apparent that the power is God's and not ours. This one reminder removes all arrogance and pride from the mission ministry of Christians. It is always God's power; it is always God's message; but people present it to other people.

It is expressed well in the chorus of a recent song entitled "People to People."

> People who know go to people who need to know Jesus;
> People who love go to people alone without Jesus;
> For there are people who need to see, people who need to love,
> People who need to know God's redeeming love.
> People who see go to those who are blind without Jesus
> And this is people to people, yes, people to people,
> All sharing together God's love.[2]

In using the various gifts that we have for mission, persons are important. In fact, the message of God's redeeming love cannot be spread without persons. Indeed, this treasure is in earthen vessels.

Possession

Each Christian possesses some gift of God's grace by the Holy Spirit. In 1 Corinthians 12:4–31 Paul describes the diversity of gifts bestowed by the Holy Spirit. Yet at the same time the church is a unity under the leadership of the Holy Spirit.

In verses 4–11 the apostle enumerated some of the gifts of the Spirit. One thing is essential to a proper understanding of both this passage and our experience: all the gifts are given by the Holy Spirit for service to the Lord. The gifts may be the possession of the individual; but they are to be used for the good of the body, the church. This is caught in *Today's English Version* translation of 1 Corinthians 12:7: "Each one is given some proof of the Spirit's presence for the good of all."

The gifts mentioned can be broadly grouped into three groups: gifts of instruction, gifts of power, and gifts of speech. Each of these spiritual gifts, or abilities, has been given by the Holy Spirit. Through the use of his gift by each person, the whole Christian community is strengthened.

The illustration of the body shows the significance of each person using his own gift. Paul employed this illustration in verses 12–26. In the human body each part, each limb, each organ has its own special function. It is not that any one of them is more important than others. One cannot have a healthy, properly functioning, perfect body without the use of each part of that body. Now certain parts may seem to be more essential than others. Certain parts may receive more attention than others. But the fact remains that the body cannot perfectly function without the use of each part.

Now apply that to the church, and especially to the mission of the church. Paul applied it in verses 27–31. God has given various persons in the church certain functions. Because some of these gifts are mentioned first in the list does not mean that they are more important than others. A church cannot properly function without preaching, teaching, administration, and evidences of the power of God. It does not really matter who does them; they must be done. And they must be done with the understanding that they are gifts of the Holy Spirit used by the individual for the good of all. The highest gift of all is the gift of love which is treated in chapter 13.

Not everyone can preach; but neither can all preachers actively seek out those in need of a Christian ministry. Not all people can teach; but neither can all teachers relate love to the "down and out" individual. Not all Christians can present an eloquent testimony; but neither can all people build a church building to be used by a mission congregation.

For several years the people of the First Baptist Church, Greenwood, Louisiana, have gone into pioneer mission areas to help construct buildings for the use of these missions and churches. People with many skills, and no particular skills, carpenters, electricians, plumbers, and those who can dig the ditches and carry the supplies to them, go together. Their wives and families go too. The women will prepare the meals and serve in mission activities. At times they have combined the trips with revivals with the pastor, George Carkeet, preaching or with surveys or Vacation Bible Schools. In a practical and tangible way each person made his own particular contribution. They have now formed an organization known as "Builders for Christ" to expand this ministry.

The principle of the use of your special gift for God's service is essential to mission action. One person may be able to teach, another to sew, another to cook, another to relate in love to all persons, another to nurse, another to comfort, and another to write letters of Christian love and concern. But each person can find the thing that he can do and can do it for God's glory.

A modest seamstress had lived out her life in a single community. She had been loyally but quietly devoted to her church. Experiencing a serious illness, she requested a visit from her pastor, a longtime friend. When the minister visited the seamstress, she shared with him this great concern: "Pastor, I know that in not too long a time my life here will be completed, and I will go to be with the Lord. I want you to know that I have no fear of death. I am greatly concerned, however, as to what I shall say when I meet the Master face to face. You know that public speaking has never been one of my gifts. How can I adequately say thank you to Jesus Christ?"

The pastor considered the woman's question. Then he gave this perceptive reply. Having known her manner of life, her steady faith, and her nimble fingers which across the years had made clothing for countless needy families, the pastor said: "I don't think you will have to say a thing. I rather think the Lord will simply say to you, 'I would like to see your hands!' "

Whatever your possession, whatever your special gift of God's Spirit, it can be used in mission. Never despair because you cannot do what another person can; neither can that person do what you can. Mission action gives an outlet for any type of skill or ability that is given to God for use.

Preparation

The person who has a gift of God's Holy Spirit in his possession is prepared for God's service. Ephesians 4:11–16 sounds something like 1 Corinthinas 12. However, there are some differences in the passages. One significant difference is the indication that the gifts given by the Holy Spirit are intended for the preparation of persons for the work of ministry.

What a difference a punctuation mark can make! The King James Version lists the functional gifts as apostles, prophets, evangelists, pastors and teachers. Then the punctuation between verses 11 and 12 make it seem to read as though one of the tasks of the ministers listed is to equip the saints, the people of God, for the ministry. Notice how it is translated in *Today's English Version* (Good News for Modern Man): "It was he who 'gave gifts to men'; he appointed some to be apostles, others to be prophets, others to be evangelists, others to be pastors and teachers. He did this to prepare all God's people for the work of Christian service, to build up the body of Christ" (Eph. 4:11–12, TEV).

While some Christians function as what we usually call our "ministers" in particular offices, their responsibility is to prepare all Christians for ministry.

Kenneth Chafin in *Help! I'm a Layman* has quoted Francis O. Ayres who wrote, "If you are a baptized Christian, you are already a minister. Whether you are ordained or not is immaterial. No matter how you react, the statement remains true. You may be surprised, alarmed, pleased, antagonized, suspicious, acquiescent, scornful, or enraged. Nevertheless, you are a minister of Christ." [3]

The apostle Paul indicated in the verses that follow that the preparation for the ministry of the Christian helps him attain the Christian maturity needed. It is only when people of God are prepared for their own ministry that they will be able to stand firm in Christ and to resist opposing doctrines and perverted teachings.

We are to be prepared for growth in Christlikeness. Verses 15 and 16 refer again to the metaphor of the body. Christ is the head. Through Christ, the whole body is made to grow and to function properly.

In the late summer of 1971 a team of eighty young people, ten physicians, and thirty-nine adult sponsors from the First Baptist Church, Pensacola, Florida, made a mission trip to the Dominican Republic. Called "Operation: Good Samaritan South" in Pensacola and *"El Coro, Por Amor, de Pensacola"* (literally, "The Chorus, For Love, of Pensacola") in the Dominican Republic, the group carried out a combination medical and musical mission. Divided into seventeen medical teams, they set up clinics in some of the poorest sections of the Dominican Republic where they treated everything from the common cold to performing cataract surgery. During the evening they performed benefit concerts to raise funds for the country's rehabilitation programs. Twice they sang in the Royal Palace before top government leaders including the president. They also performed in city squares and on television before thousands of Dominican people.

The pastor, James Pleitz, reported that the project began more than a year earlier when the church began thinking of ways to get youth and others involved in helping people in need. This was not intended as just one mission project. Paul Royal, minister of music and coordinator of the project said, "They felt to the man that in order for us to enjoy the integrity of proclaiming the reason we did this, we must carry out the same sort of ministry, the same sort of sharing right here in Pensacola." [4]

Christians can be prepared for their own ministry. This makes us mature, stable believers. This enables us to use the various gifts that we might have for mission.

Production

God expects production from us. We are not simply to sit back and enjoy all the blessings of the Christian faith. Neither are we just to sit around and become saturated with study. Both the study and the meaning of our faith are intended to enable us to produce for Christ.

Buckner Fanning related in *Christ in Your Shoes* that a deacon friend of his caught the idea that a Christian should produce. They were going back home from a retreat in the hill country of Texas. Fanning said to him, "Man, wasn't that a terrific retreat?" He was bulging with notes, sermon ideas, illustrations, and the good food they had eaten.

His friend's reply was neither cynical nor bitter; he was just being honest. He said. "Yeah, Buckner, it was good, but I want to tell you something. I've had all the inspiration I can stand. I've taken my last note. I've remembered my last point. I've been importing and I am satiated. I have been receiving, I have been taking in, I have been getting ideas, I have been getting inspiration. I'm through. Buckner, unless you and/or the church can give me a handle whereby I can start translating some of these ideas, this concern, and this inspiration into some practical deeds of Christian ministry, I've had it." [5]

In a little parable found in Luke 13:6–9 Jesus also indicated that we are intended to produce. The story concerned a man who had a fig tree in his vineyard. For three years the tree had not produced figs so the man told his vinedresser to cut it down. The vinedresser pleaded for just one more year. Then after the care given to it for one more year he would remove the tree if it still did not produce.

The tree's whole problem was that it had done nothing. It was considered capable of producing fruit; but it had not. This is a parable of judgment and is, of course, primarily directed to Israel. But Christians can surely apply it.

Since we have been given various gifts we must use these gifts for mission. The Savior expects us to produce a ministry. We must be productive for him.

Purpose

Illustrative material used by Paul in Ephesians 5:22–27 serves to demonstrate to us the purpose of the church. The key verse is Ephesians 5:21 where Paul tells believers to be submissive to one another. Then he applied it to family relationships. The primary reference is to domestic relations. The illustrative material involves the church and in the process tells us something of what Christ intended for his church.

The wife is to be submissive to her husband as the church submits itself to Christ. Christ is the head of the church. The church must always be submissive to Christ and responsive to him.

The husband is to love his wife as Christ loved the church. How much did Christ love the church? He loved it enough to give himself in sacrifice for it. By his death for the church, for the people who compose the church, Christ dedicated the church to God. This is indeed a strong love.

Another significant expression showed the purpose of Christ in dying for the church, sanctifying it for God, and cleansing it. This was done "in order to present the church to himself, in all its beauty, pure and faultless, without spot or wrinkle, or any other imperfection" (Eph. 5:27, TEV).

Apart from what Christ has already done for the church by his death and by his setting it apart, the church becomes "pure and spotless" when it carries out Christ's purpose.

Christ's purpose for the church is mission. Mission cannot be conducted unless all the components of the church, its members, use the various gifts that God has given to them in mission. The real importance is not the type of the gift but the use of the gift.

A church is composed of persons who have been redeemed by Christ. Not only have they been redeemed they have been equipped by the gifts of the Holy Spirit. These gifts, whatever they may be, must be used in mission. This is their purpose.

9

Involved in Mission

Acts 4:32–37; 5:1–11; 8:1–8

In his book *Christ in Your Shoes* Buckner Fanning tells the story of Mrs. Kamila Michowski of Warsaw, Poland. When he first met her in 1969 in the Baptist church in Warsaw, she was ninety years old. During the German occupation of Poland during World War II, Hitler had pushed a half million Jews into a ghetto in which forty thousand people had lived. Fifty thousand of them died the first month. Mrs. Michowski, a Christian, jeopardized her life by putting on a Star of David armband and going into the Jewish ghetto. Thus identifying herself with the people in their critical hour of need she would smuggle bread and Bibles into the ghetto, always the two—bread and Bibles. She would distribute a loaf of bread and the Living Bread. Over a hundred people were introduced to faith in Christ because of the bread and the Bibles. She was involved in mission.[1]

Every believer should be involved in mission. Perhaps missions has been defined too narrowly at times. If one were not a career missionary serving either in a foreign field or a home field, or if he were not an active member of a mission organization, he was not thought to be involved in missions. Mission involvement has been considered as professional or institutional rather than as personal.

The early Christians, however, were all involved in mission. Modern Christians, too, must be involved in mission. When missions is defined as the presentation of the gospel in various forms, this does not seem an impossible task. Look again, if you will, at some of the activities of the earliest Christians. It will become apparent that they were involved in mission. This is our goal, too: that we might all become involved in mission. Involvement makes missions become real and personal to us.

Dedication

The measure of the dedication of these Christians to one another and to the mission task is seen in one decisive action. Acts 4:32–37 records the dedication of their goods to the common good due to their dedication to God and to one another.

The depth of Christian fellowship and the genuineness of Christian concern were the motivating factors in their actions. It is said that those who believed were "of one heart and of one soul" (Acts 4:32). Unity of this kind produces the desire to help those who might have need.

So dedicated were they to the relief of their needs that they did not selfishly consider their possessions their own. Each person was willing to share with others. It is indicated that none of them had needs that the others did not help to meet.

Possessions were sold and the proceeds were given to the apostles. This was then distributed according to the needs of the believers.

One person particularly was mentioned. His name was Barnabas; he was known as the "son of consolation." So consoling were his nature and his activities that he became popularly known by this name.

Some modern Christians get upset and edgy when they read this passage. The immediate reaction is that this is a communistic or socialistic action and that we ought to explain it. At times there is a little embarrassment over it. But when the passage is examined, the differences become pronounced. This was not a matter of legislation but love; this was not due to the power of the state but the state of the heart; this was not forced but spontaneous; this did not equalize but empathized as each felt very deeply the needs of others.

The only explanation necessary is that there was such a sharing of the common life that each felt a responsibility for the others. This awoke in them a real desire to share all that they had. So the people did not consider what they had exclusively their own but had all things in common and shared as others had need. Dedication of self and dedication of goods were the determinative factors.

The results of their actions were significant. Notice: "And with great power the apostles gave their testimony to the resurrection of the Lord Jesus, and great grace was upon them all" (Acts 4:33, RSV).

These people had created such an atmosphere of love, concern, dedication, mission, and ministry that the Holy Spirit was able to work decisively. The power of God was reflected in the power of their lives.

So often we contemporary Christians consider our possessions to be ours alone. We do not exhibit either the dedication or the desire to share these with others in their need.

It starts with material possessions. Things that others could use are selfishly hoarded or willfully wasted. A missionary who was home on furlough was invited to a dinner at a summer resort where he met many women of prominence and position. Later he wrote his wife: "Dear Wife: I've had dinner at the hotel. The company was wonderful. I saw strange things today. Many women were present, and some of them to my certain knowledge wore a church, forty cottage organs, and twenty libraries." In his desire to present the gospel to those among whom he ministered he could not refrain from looking at the things around him in terms of human need. This the early believers did in their dedication; this we often fail to do.

The dedication of self to mission includes time, too. Quite often the most important thing a person can give is time. A parent may give his child many things, but if he does not give him time he still has very little. Simply giving your money is not necessarily the best way to practice missions even though it is the easiest. The time that it takes to tutor a child, to man a "hot line" and talk to someone in trouble, to prepare and serve a meal, to organize a game, or to just listen and be a friend may be your greatest investments.

And you cannot get away from talents when you consider dedication. These do not have to be the spectacular talents. The simple talents can be used by God for mission when they are dedicated to him. The junior-high Acteens in the First Baptist Church, Natchitoches, Louisiana, planned and prepared a "back-to-school" wardrobe for some younger disadvantaged Negro girls. Sewing seems a simple talent. But it can be used in mission.

The presentation of the gospel in power and the dedication to meeting human need go together. After a fierce battle, a chaplain walked out upon the battlefield with his Bible under his arm. He found a boy who was wounded and dying. "Would you like for me to read you something out of the Book?" asked the chaplain. The boy replied, "I am so thirsty, I would rather have a drink of water." The chaplain hurried off and soon returned with water. Then the boy said, "Could you lift my head and put something under it?" The chaplain took off his own overcoat, rolled it up and placed it as a comfortable pillow under the boy's head. Then the boy said, "I'm so cold, I wish I had something over me." The chaplain took off his other coat and wrapped it around the boy. Then the boy looked up into his face and said, "O sir, if there is anything in that Book which makes a man do for another what you have done for me, let me hear it."

Deceit

It is not necessary to add that all Christians are not involved in mission. Immediately following the passage that relates the sharing concern of the early Christians the terrible account of a deceitful action is reported. Since they follow one on the heels of the other, it seems as though the actions of Barnabas and Ananias were contrasted.

Ananias also owned a piece of property. This he sold and brought a portion of the proceeds to the apostles. When he presented the money to Peter, he indicated that it was the total proceeds from the sale. The story is told in Acts 5:1–11.

Peter knew that this was a falsehood. He chided Ananias for his action. The pooling of resources had been voluntary acts. He did not have to sell it. Neither did he have to give the total proceeds from the sale. But he had misrepresented his action. He had made the Holy Spirit a party to his crime since he apparently had said that what he had done was under the leadership of the Holy Spirit.

Whether it was from fright, from shock, or as a judgment of God is not clear, but Ananias died immediately following Peter's remonstrance. Likely it was from fright; but those around obviously interpreted it as the judgment of God upon him.

Three hours later Sapphira, his wife, came to Peter. Upon being questioned, she answered with the same statements Ananias had made. Peter then warned her of the enormity of their deceit. He told her that those who had buried her husband were just then returning. She died too.

Their problem was one of misrepresentation. Apparently they were eager to reap the benefits from an alleged generosity. But they were deceitful in their actions. What was worse, they involved the Holy Spirit in their crime.

Even in mission action motives need to be constantly examined. Is a project conceived because of the good that it can do others, or because of the fame it can bring the originators? Is an action practiced because of genuine concern or because of a reputation that is desired? Was the Holy Spirit really behind an idea, or was it an attempt at self-glorification? Was the goal the good of the people, or the completion of the report? Was the work really wholehearted, or did the credit received make the work seem more significant than it really was?

The Christian community had made no demand upon Ananias and Sapphira for the sale of their land. They would likely have been pleased with any portion of the proceeds that they were given. But this couple desired recognition that was out of proportion to their contribution. They wanted the credit of being known as sacrificial givers who gave all, when actually they had only given a part. Rather than looking at the situation in terms of human need, they had looked at it in terms of self-aggrandizement.

This experience serves as a constant reminder to all: Christian mission and ministry is not to be taken lightly. It is better not to attempt it at all than to attempt to gain recognition for self and a reputation for service at the expense of true concern. It becomes even more serious when an attempt is made to involve God in our failures by ascribing them to him.

The ideal is for all Christians to be involved in mission. The actual situation is that we failed to become actively involved.

I once led a seminar on Christian witnessing at a Louisiana Baptist student convention. During the course of the discussion I quoted Alan Richardson who had described the gospel as "hot potato news." Then I attempted to explain the quotation. I said, "Suppose you were out camping and had cooked your meal over an open fire. Someone reached in the coals and pulled out a potato wrapped in aluminum foil and tossed it to you. What would you do?" Very quickly a girl sitting on the front row said, "I would drop it."

She surely ruined that illustration! What I was driving at was that one does not just stand around holding a hot potato. He passes it on—or does something with it. But probably that girl's illustration was better than mine. That is what happens too often. We have been given a mission to complete. But rather than being involved in mission, often the hot potato is dropped, and we fail.

Determination

Turn now from a negative statement to a positive attitude. Ananias and Sapphira failed to become involved in mission. They were deceitful and their deceit made an unhappy story.

Fortunately that was far from the whole story. Most of the early believers were determined to witness for Christ and to become involved in mission. This made an exciting story.

Turn in your Bible to Acts 8:1–8. The scene seems dark. It is a time of persecution. After the death of Stephen, who was the first Christian martyr, Paul (then known as Saul) was making havoc of the church. Persecution was intent. As an angry boar would tear up a garden spot, Paul was disturbing the Christians.

As a result the believers scattered. The Bible records, "They were all scattered abroad throughout the regions of Judaea and Samaria" (Acts 8:1).

But the scene was not really as dark as it seemed. Notice another statement: "Therefore they that were scattered abroad went everywhere preaching the word" (Acts 8:4). Our immediate reaction is to say that these were the apostles who were preaching in other areas. After all, they were the leaders and would likely be the first to leave. But read Acts 8:1 again, "They were all scattered abroad throughout the regions of Judaea and Samaria, *except the apostles* (italics mine)." So it was not the apostles who preached the word, witnessed for Christ, who became involved in mission, in the regions to which they were scattered. It was the lay people; they were the ordinary Christians. They were men and women who were so involved in mission that even when they were displaced from their homes and their normal activities they continued to witness.

One cannot help but wonder how much effect their expulsion had on their witness. They were forced to leave their homes, their familiar surroundings, their normal routine. When they were away from these places they became effective witnesses.

Perhaps that is what we need to become involved in witness: to leave our comfortable, familiar surroundings. For anyone to become involved in mission he may have to move some. He may need to go into another area to minister to human need. He may have to leave his comfortable home to go to a neighborhood service center, a mission building that is not so nice and neat, or into the streets where people are. It is not too often that mission and ministry can be conducted in comfort and convenience.

And there may be times that the expulsion is not physical but mental. It may be that a new attitude, a new way of looking at a situation will have to be developed. What had not seemed a mission opportunity previously may turn out to be the most exciting and accessible mission opportunity available.

Several years ago at a Southern Baptist Convention Pastor's Conference one of the speakers mentioned a young businessman who had made a startling discovery. The businessman had said: "All this past year I have been telling my wife that my job was my problem. That by the time I spent all week in the atmosphere of that office with all of the things that were done and said completely foreign to my own way of life— by the weekend I was in no frame of mind to teach my Sunday School Class." Then he continued: "But now I have come to the marvelous realization that my job is not my problem but my parish. Now each morning I can't wait until I get down to the office and see what God is going to do for somebody that day."

Going out into the world is not all there is to it. When the Christian goes out into the world, he is to go with the gospel. These people went "preaching the word." A verbal explanation of Christ is essential. As the Christian is expelled from his home, his office, his church, or his class or circle into the world he goes with a message. It is the message of Christ.

One man is isolated as an example. Philip went to Samaria, then later he went toward Gaza, and then later he went to the Mediterranean seacoast until he reached Caesarea. These are all mentioned in Acts 8. And each place he proclaimed Christ as Savior.

Samuel Shoemaker summarized the importance of the verbal witness in mission. He said: "I cannot, by being good, tell men of Jesus' atoning death and resurrection, nor of my faith in His divinity. The emphasis is too much on me and too little on Him. Our lives must be made as consistent as we can make them with our faith; but our faith, if we are Christians, is vastly greater than our lives. That is why the 'word' of witness is so important." [2]

An important outcome is evident when Christians are determined to become involved in mission. After Philip had ministered in Samaria and many people had been blessed by his ministry, the Scripture notes, "And there was great joy in that city" (Acts 8:8). Joy is the outcome of determined Christian mission.

Joy is twofold in its outreach. There is joy on the part of those who have been the recipients of Christian mission. Now that they know Christ and their lives have been touched by Christian love they have joy. Any kind of practical Christian mission that helps another creates joy of some kind in the person helped. But there is also joy on the part of the one who has ministered. While not done selfishly in order to create a spirit of joy, joy is a natural outcome of mission.

Would it not be great if all Christians were involved in mission? That is our calling. That is our ideal. The early Christians seemed to do it. With effort and motivation modern Christians can do it too.

10.
Broadening Concepts in Mission

Acts 10—11; 13:1–3; 1 Corinthians 9:19–22; 16:9

That we live in a changing world is quite obvious. Also obvious is the understanding that new times demand new responses.

Albert McClellan, program planning secretary of the Executive Committee, Southern Baptist Convention, has been one of the writers who has alerted us to the extent of the change and to the challenge of that change to the churches. He wrote in *The New Times* published in 1968:

> With God's help man has made the tools that have changed the face of the earth. . . . What started out to be a tiny trickle of change, proceeding slowly and imperceptibly at times, has now, in the twentieth century, emerged as a furious whirlpool of change that threatens the stability of the race. . . . In a way man has done quite well with his challenge, and what he has done has shaped his personal future. It has made him something quite different from what he was in the Garden of Eden and different from what he was a generation ago. The purpose of this book is to show some of these changes and their effect on future man and to show that in turn the changes have altered the processes of the Christian mission.[1]

The significant statement for us at this time is that the changes of our world have "altered the processes of the Christian mission."

But we are not the first generation to face changed conditions. It also happened right at the beginning of the Christian era. The early disciples had stuck close to Christ. Then Christ was crucified. After which he was resurrected from the dead and ultimately he ascended to be with the father. How this changed their situation!

On the day of Pentecost the believers were filled with the power of the Holy Spirit and began an active witness. Persecution was their lot. For the most part in those early days they confined their activities to the Jews. They were in real danger of becoming simply another sect of Judaism.

But God propelled these followers of Jesus out. In a series of events it became clear that the mission of the church was to all the world. In one way after another they came to have broadening concepts of mission. They came to understand that Gentiles could be saved too. Not only could Gentiles be saved but the followers were to actively seek to bring the Gentiles to an understanding of God. Suddenly it must have become apparent to them that they faced a whole new world. Their concepts of mission had to be broadened.

Notice some of the events that led to the broadening concepts of mission. Tentative steps they were at first. But each one helped the cause of Christ to advance to a fuller understanding of missions.

In our day of breathtaking change we can gain guidance from these events. If we are to be the church in mission in our day some broadened concepts of mission will be demanded.

Attitude

Basic in our broadened concept of mission is a change in attitude. For many people changes in attitude are necessary before any change in action can be realized.

Simon Peter had to have a change in attitude before he could begin a ministry to Gentiles. The story is told in Acts 10:1 to 11:18.

Peter was visiting in the home of Simon, a tanner, at Joppa. At some time before noon he went to the flat roof of the house to pray and to wait for lunch. While there, he apparently fell asleep. In his sleep he had a dream in which he saw a sheet descending from heaven filled with animals and birds. The command was, "Rise,

Peter; kill and eat" (Acts 10:13, RSV). His response was, "No, Lord; for I have never eaten anything that is common or unclean" (Acts 10:14, RSV). Then came the reply, "What God has cleansed, you must not call common" (Acts 10:15, RSV). Three times this occurred before Peter was awakened.

This dream was a preparation for Simon Peter. The preceding day a Roman centurion (a military leader in charge of one hundred men) also saw a vision from God. Cornelius was a God-fearer. While not a full proselyte to Judaism, he believed in God and was very beneficent to the Jews. In the vision he was told that his activities had been pleasing to God. At Joppa he would find Simon Peter at the home of Simon the tanner. He was instructed to send to Joppa for Peter.

While Peter was trying to interpret his dream, the men from Cornelius arrived. On an impulse from the Holy Spirit, Peter identified himself to these men, invited them into the house to be his guest; and then the next day went with them to Caesarea.

Accompanied by some Christians from Joppa, Peter found Cornelius waiting for him with some friends and relatives. Cornelius fell before him, but Peter urged him to get up, reminding Cornelius that he was only a man.

Peter began almost half apologetic for being there. He said: "You yourselves know very well that a Jew is not allowed by his religion to visit or associate with a Gentile. But God has shown me that I must not consider any man unclean or defiled. And so when you sent for me I came without objection. I ask you, then, why did you send for me?" (Acts 10:28–29, TEV).

Cornelius then explained to Peter his experience in prayer. Beginning with the significant words, "I now realize that it is true that God treats all men alike. Whoever fears him and does what is right is acceptable to him, no matter what race he belongs to" (Acts 10:34–35, TEV), Peter preached to them.

In the midst of Peter's message they received Christ. Upon

receiving Christ they also received the Holy Spirit; it was evident through visible signs.

Peter, the Jew who had been convinced that Gentiles were unclean, had changed his attitude. Through the demonstration of God's grace and power his attitude had been changed. He now knew that God and his salvation were intended for all people.

First Baptist Church, Dallas, Texas, is the largest church cooperating with the Southern Baptist Convention. For many years this church pursued a vigorous missions program to minority groups, but it was understood that the local church was closed to membership to local Negroes. The pastor, W. A. Criswell, had been identified with a segregationist stance. But then he was elected president of the Southern Baptist Convention in 1968. Upon returning to Dallas he met with the deacons of the church then preached a strong sermon the following Sunday entitled "The Church of the Open Door." In this sermon he told of his change of mind and asked the church to assume an open door policy for church membership. This they did.

In his sermon he said:

> So I said to those Deacons, that as for me, and my heart, and my life, and my pulpit ministry, I am done with the emptiness of an appeal preached in fear that somebody of a different pigment might accept it and come forward. . . . Not in dramatics, not in fanfare, but in the spirit of Jesus, humbly, and simply I declare that the First Baptist Church of Dallas is now and forever a Philadelphian Church of the Open Door. Anybody can come—anybody, and may God bless him and God attend him in the way as he comes. . . .This is a church of the Open Door and we turn and face the world, our gospel shall be to all men everywhere.[2]

All the believers did not have the experience of Peter. When he returned to Jerusalem, those who were of a Judaistic group desiring Christians to first become Jews criticized Peter. Patiently he explained to them what had happened. His report was corroborated by those who had gone with him. After hearing the complete report, they "stopped their criticism and praised God, saying, 'Then God has given to the Gentiles also the opportunity to repent and live' " (Acts 11:18, TEV).

What a change of attitude this was! The concept of mission had been broadened. No one was outside the scope of God's love.

Acceptance

With the understanding that God loved all men and that salvation was for all people, the next step in the broadening concept of mission is the acceptance of the task. To be willing to accept all people is one thing; to actively seek to bring them to Christ is another thing altogether.

But the pioneering Christians were willing to do this. It was not in Jerusalem, however, but in Antoich that this was first done. Read Acts 11:19–26 and Acts 13:1–3 for this thrilling story of mission advance.

The breakthrough of preaching the gospel to the Gentiles occurred at Antioch. When the news of this filtered back to Jerusalem, the church at Jerusalem sent Barnabas to investigate the situation. Barnabas was thrilled with what he had found. He then sent to Tarsus for Paul. Together Barnabas and Paul preached and taught in Antioch.

There may be some significance that it was at Antioch that the believers were first called Christians. At that place they had so caught the spirit of Christ that they could be known as the Christ-people, the Christians.

And it was from Antioch that the first organized Christian mission activity was begun. Some of the church leaders received the message from the Holy Spirit to separate Barnabas and Paul to a special work.

So after a period of fasting and praying they laid their hands upon them, commissioning them for the missionary task.

Acceptance of the broadening concept of mission had come. It was not enough just to know that God would save them. Neither was it just enough to be willing to witness to others. New methods had to be tried to carry the message of Christ and his love. The missionary journey was one new method.

A new method tried by the Willow Meadows Baptist Church, Houston, Texas, was the "Heart of Houston" Project. Willow Meadows Baptist Church is a suburban church. Growing out of the shocking realization of the fifteen and sixteen-year-old group of the conditions in the inner city, a unique program of ministry was begun. Rather than carrying supplies and personnel to the inner city for a mission project they bussed children from the inner city to the church. Using the church facilities, they provided Bible study taught by teen-aged teachers who had been trained on Sunday evenings. It was discovered that many of the children came to church hungry, so a snack was provided for them. On Tuesday afternoons they were bussed to the church for a program of music, recreation, and a hot meal, for some the only hot meal of the week. The teen-aged missionaries became ministers throughout the week and not just on Sundays and Tuesdays through their contacts with these children and their families. The racial make-up of the children involved was about two-thirds Negro and one-third Latin American.

About the results of this mission method Ralph A. Langley, the pastor, wrote:

> Something began to happen with our own church with this direct missions involvement. For instance, there was new life immediately for some in our WMU. . . .Other units and organizations in our church have been spiritually quickened by this missions action program. Some have volunteered time, some have contributed money, others have given their solid encouragement and support. The most remarkable sign of all has been the reduced suspicion and prejudice across racial lines—reminding us hopefully of the theme of the book

of Ephesians of the breaking down of the middle wall of partition between the races.[3]

Broadening concepts of mission mean the acceptance of new methods for presenting the concern and compassion of Christ.

Approach

Paul gave a hint as to his approach to the presentation of the gospel. In 1 Corinthians 9:19–22 he testified:

> I am a free man, nobody's slave; but I make myself everybody's slave in order to win as many as possible. While working with the Jews, I live like a Jew in order to win them; and even though I myself am not subject to the Law of Moses, I live as though I were, when working with those who are, in order to win them. In the same way, when with Gentiles I live like a Gentile, outside the Jewish Law, in order to win Gentiles. This does not mean that I don't obey God's law, for I am really under Christ's law. Among the weak in faith I become weak like one of them, in order to win them. So I become all things to all men, that I may save some of them by any means possible (TEV).

By this Paul certainly did not mean that he had become so unprincipled that he had no convictions. He was not so fluid that he could switch from one position to another with ease. Rather, it meant that he was willing to identify himself with all men in order to reach them with the redeeming message of Christ. Where no principle was involved, he could identify with the person in his situation. He would relate to people where they were.

This is a valid mission approach. Christian mission must be neither patronizing nor condescending. The witness for Christ must be able to relate to the person with whom he is working. This is the reason that Christian witness often starts with a meal, some clothing, help with school lessons, or instruction in child care before the message is ever shared. This approach will mean that many times sermons are lived before they are ever preached.

Jim Reid resigned the pastorate of the Faith Baptist Church, Las Vegas, Nevada, to begin an unofficial ministry to the "Strip" in Las Vegas. Now under appointment by the Home Mission Board of the Southern Baptist Convention he conducts Bible studies, leads a Sunday afternoon worship service in a hotel, and teaches English classes to show people who do not speak English. He relates to people there by his dress and by his accommodation to their working hours. He has begun to mingle freely with the stage hands, pit bosses, and bartenders. He began his ministry by simply developing friendships with the show people. Through entering into conversation with them he was able to establish the rapport that led to Bible studies and worship services. He had adopted Paul's approach to missions.[4]

Broadening concepts in mission will open the doors to new approaches. But these approaches will have to be based on identification with the people with whom we minister and relating to them personally. The personal touch can never be neglected.

Adversaries

Broadened concepts of mission will likely bring some resistance and opposition. The anticipation of opposition should not deter one from mission activity, however, if he is convinced that this is God's work and God's will.

In closing the first letter to the Corinthian Christians Paul said, "I plan to stay here in Ephesus until the day of Pentecost. There is a real opportunity here for great and worth-while work, even though there are many opponents" (1 Cor. 16:8–9, TEV).

Paul seemed to relate the opportunities with the opposition. Simply because he anticipated some opposition was no reason to flee the opportunity that God had placed before him.

That is nearly always the case. All people have not had the same experiences; they have not come to the same understanding; they have not all developed the same perspective. This does not mean that new mission concepts should be abandoned. It may mean that the basis for them should be studied carefully and the plans developed thoroughly. Then if the conviction is still present that it is God's way to work in that situation at that time proceed with mission action.

At Ephesus a strong church was developed. Paul had faced opposition there. A riot had been incited due to the cry of the silversmiths that Paul's preaching would ruin the market for their idols of Diana whose temple was located there. But in the face of the opposition was also the opportunity to allow the broadened concepts of mission to come to fruition.

Opposition can come from two sources: within and without. The forces from without are those that would resist the spread of the gospel. They are the situations that would make mission difficult in that place. The opposition from within are those who would not feel that the methods were proper. Perhaps they are not quite ready for new methods and new approaches. Even William Carey had to face this kind of opposition. Adversaries to mission action may always be present.

These are changing times. But in these changing times themselves are to be found the greatest opportunities for mission yet to be faced by the churches. But to take advantage of it broadened concepts of mission must be necessary. J. Wallace Hamilton was right when he said, "The upsetness of our time is not so much our problem as it is our chance—an open door the Lord has set before us." [5]

11.

Metaphors of Mission

Mark 10:45; John 1:12; Acts 1:5; 12:4–21; Romans 12:4; 2 Corinthians 6:16; 13:4; Galatians 4:21–31; Ephesians 2:11–22; 1 Peter 2:9–11; Revelation 19:7–9

How do you describe a church? Obviously it is not described simply by the building in which it meets. It possibly can be described by the functions it performs. But it must also be described by some objective reality which it is. In order to make these descriptions, however, we have to depend on metaphors.

Frederick B. Speakman's Jack Wilson in *God and Jack Wilson* answered a critic of the church by saying:

> The real church . . . is nothing less than the laboratory of the new community of mankind which God's love through Christ keeps trying to shape humanity into. It is nothing less than the laboratory of a God-created community, called into this world by Him and depending on Him for all its life and energy. . . .
>
> It's as if with each generation, right in the teeth of whatever's threatening humanity the worst, the Master Conductor is calling together another ragtag orchestra of amateur musicians and asking us to play music that's so great we can't quite play it! Yet, in the very trying and for all our bungling, for all the discordant sound of our efforts, some things get done for God in our time. Some things get done for Christ that, without the church, wouldn't get done.[1]

We are not the first persons to resort to metaphors to describe the church. The biblical writers did it too. Throughout the New Testament a number of metaphors have been used to describe the church. (One New Testament scholar has counted nearly one hundred!)

An interesting feature of these metaphors is that they can also be used as metaphors of mission. Not only do they help us understand the nature of the church, they also help us describe the mission of the church.

We will make no attempt to exhaust the metaphors of mission found in the New Testament. Look at half a dozen of the most significant. Consider how these metaphors can aid both your understanding of the nature of the church and the mission of the church.

The People of God

In 1 Peter 2:1–11 reference is made to the "people of God." This concept links the New Testament church with the Old Testament community of faith.

God had made a covenant with the people of Israel. He would be their God and would give them guidance and protection; they would be his people and would give to him faithfulness and obedience. They were the people of God.

But in Jesus Christ God had made a new and complete covenant. By Christ's death on the cross atonement was made for the sins of man. Those who accepted Christ became the sons of God. In beautifully expressive language 1 Peter 2:10 states what has happened: "At one time you were not God's people, but now you are his people; at one time you did not know God's mercy, but now you have received his mercy" (TEV).

As the people of God, the church is to carry on the work of God. Being identified with God would indicate an attempt to live and to express the will of God in this world. The people of God must be consistent with the character and the concern of God.

Christ wept over the city of Jerusalem at its rejection of the prophets of God. He was moved with compassion when he saw the leaderless people. He acted out of love and healed the sick, raised the dead, and fed the hungry. What should be the reaction of Christ's people to unconcern, lack of coordination and direction, hunger, poverty, and loneliness today? How would Christ act in our place?

Often the story has been repeated of the businessman scurrying along the railroad track in the terminal to catch a train that was soon to depart. In his haste he knocked over a table on which a crippled body had set up small merchandise to sell: pencils, shoelaces, razor blades, and assorted items. Without stopping to pick up the goods or the boy who had been knocked off his stool he continued his race to the train. Behind him came another equally rushed passenger who stopped, righted the stool and placed the boy on it, picked up the scattered merchandise, gave the boy some money to cover any loss, and then rushed toward his departing train. After he had moved down the track a little way the boy shouted after him: "Hey, mister. Hey, mister. Are you Jesus Christ?" At which the man halted, turned to the boy, and replied: "No, son, I'm not. I'm just one of his followers who is trying to live like he would." That is what it means to be a part of the people of God.

You will notice from 1 Peter 2:11 that the people of God are a pilgrim people. Their citizenship is on earth but their home is heaven.

Pilgrims are always in search. They are in transit to another place. As the people of God, Christians must always be in search of God's will and effective ways of service. It is too easy to settle in and become a settler rather than a pilgrim. But the compulsion of the Holy Spirit and compassion from the Holy Spirit cause the people of God to be pilgrims searching for their mission in the world.

A Royal Priesthood

In 1 Peter the same concept that was applied to the people of Israel in Deuteronomy 19 is applied to the new people of God. Among other things in 1 Peter 2:9 the church is called a "royal priesthood."

The function of a priest is to serve as a means for others to find God. As the people of Israel were to fulfill a priestly role in the world by pointing others to God, so is the church.

We have often considered the idea of the "priesthood of believers" simply in personal terms. Each man can be his own priest. Each person can approach God directly. We do not have to use intermediaries in order to come before God. But we should also consider the priesthood of the believers in corporate terms. We are to serve as priests in this world. Not only are we able to approach God directly, but we are also to help others to know God. Our priesthood is not an end in itself; it is also a means.

The implications of the royal priesthood for mission are overwhelming. It would indicate that this is an essential function of the Christian church. It does not have to be done through ritual. It can be done in the various ways that a person or a group of persons can reflect the love of God and point others to the knowledge of God.

The Body of Christ

It is impossible for us to think of a person without a body. In the days of the incarnation Jesus had a body. The Scripture considers the church to be the body of Christ.

Notice Ephesians 4:4 and Romans 12:4. In both these references the believers are called the body of Christ.

Christ must be the head of the body. As the human body responds to the signals given by the brain which is located in the head, so the Christian body must respond to Christ.

All the members of the body serve the entire body. In the discussion that follows in Romans 12 Paul made that explicit. Different members of the body might have different gifts and different abilities. Yet each of them are significant for the whole. The body cannot exist without each part doing its part.

The metaphor of the church as the body of Christ emphasizes the common life that we have in Christ. It was in Christ that we found life and it is in Christ that we are called to live together. We become one body of believers seeking to follow his will and to serve his needs.

Without the concept of body there can be little mission. Each individual member may not be able to perform the same function; but each can perform his function. It does not matter that one task may not seem as glamorous as others. Each counts.

Related to the idea of the church as the body of Christ is the concept of the household of God. In John 1:12; Romans 8:15; and Galatians 6:10 are found references to the household of God. The household of God is composed of all those who know God in salvation and faith. To be a part of the household of God is to have become a part of the body of Christ by faith. Children of God are both members of the household of God and contributing parts of the body of Christ.

The Bride of Christ

The church has sometimes been called the bride of Christ. Primary to this understanding is the section in Revelation 19:6–9 which describes the marriage of the church and the lamb. The church has kept its robes clean in faithfulness to God even in times of severe trial. All the redeemed are pictured as having been invited to attend the marriage feast.

Basic to this understanding is the complete union between Christ and the church. In biblical language when two persons are married the two become one. The union between Christ and his church is complete. In several Old Testament references the prophets likened Israel to an unfaithful wife. The old people of God had been unfaithful to God. With the new relationship that the people of God have with God through Christ, a faithful union between God and the people of God is anticipated.

In Galatians 4:21–31 Paul resorted to allegory to express the freedom of the Christian. He drew the distinction between those under the law and those under Christ as the distinction between Abraham's son by Hagar (Ishmael) and his son by Sarah (Isaac). This is a type of interpretation that is strange to us but was common to the first-century Jewish rabbis. Christians are the children of promise. God promised Abraham and Sarah that they would have a son. It seemed an impossibility. But God's promise was fulfilled. The greatest of all God's promises was the promise of Christ and salvation through Christ. This, too, he has delivered. The church is the descendent of the free woman.

Ephesians 5:21–23 is a clearer expression of the figure of the church as the bride of Christ. In this passage the teachings about husbands and wives and the church and Christ are intermingled. Wives are to be subject to their husbands as the church is subject to Christ. Husbands are to love their wives as Christ loved the church and gave himself for it. The relationship between Christ and the church stands as the example of a proper relationship between husbands and wives. Christ loved the church. The church is submissive to Christ.

The obvious implication for mission from this metaphor is submission to the will of God. The church must always be submissive to God's will. God's will might lead into absolutely new areas of mission. Consider a ministry to the aging, for instance. Perhaps the church had not really considered that its problem. But under the leadership of the Holy Spirit it has become apparent that the church can minister in many ways to the aging. It could do so with a club which offers fellowship periodically, a craft program, a network that calls daily to those who live alone, a "meal on wheels" program to see that they have at least one hot meal a day, help in transportation problems, or simply someone to be a friend to a lonely and forgotten person.

If the church is truly the bride of Christ, then it should be submissive to Christ even as a bride is submissive to her loving husband.

A Community of the Spirit

The one thing that sets the church apart from just any voluntary group of persons is the presence and power of the Holy Spirit. The Holy Spirit transforms a collection of persons into a fellowship of Christians.

Before the ascension Jesus told his followers to wait in Jerusalem until they received the promised Spirit. John had baptized them with water but they would be immersed in the Holy Spirit (Acts 1:5). This was accomplished at the day of Pentecost. The Holy Spirit came upon them with power and they were transformed.

In both 2 Corinthians 13:14 and Philippians 2:1 Paul mentioned the "fellowship of the Spirit." It is the fellowship of the Spirit that creates the community of the Spirit. The Holy Spirit gives life and sanctification to the believer. He gives power and purpose through his presence. Without the fellowship of the Spirit there could be no community of the Spirit.

Related to this is the expression of the church as the temple of God. The Temple was considered the dwelling place of God. God now dwells in the lives of his followers. The claim is boldly stated in 2 Corinthians 6:16 that the Christians are the temple of the living God. This is where God is, in a community of the Spirit called forth by his grace.

The same thought is carried further in Ephesians 2:11–22. An analogy was drawn to the old Temple with its various courts for women, for Gentiles, and for men. In Christ the dividing partitions were demolished. Through the power of the Holy Spirit, God has created a new person, a Christian person. Then he builds of these new people a temple, a dwelling place of God. It is the fellowship of the Spirit that makes the Christian person the dwelling place of God's Spirit.

So the church can be considered a community of the Spirit. The Holy Spirit gives it life, infills it, and empowers it. With a sense of community the church moves into its mission in the world. Acts of mercy and mission are not isolated, unrelated acts, but a result of the sense of community that feels an obligation to all people.

The Servants of God

Perhaps the most familiar figure of Jesus in the New Testament is as the servant of God. Identifying with the servant passages in Isaiah, Jesus made it known that he had come to serve. Throughout the Gospels he is found pouring out his life in service to others. He even gave service as a summary statement of his purpose: "For even the Son of Man did not come to be served: he came to serve and to give his life to redeem many people" (Mark 10:45, TEV).

If the church identifies itself with Christ then it, too, must be a servant church. The church exists as the servant of God.

As E. Glenn Hinson has written in *The Church Design for Survival:* the church "exists in order to pour out its life in service— healing the sick, casting out demons, cleansing lepers, restoring sight for the blind, providing food for the hungry, giving rest to the weary, making homes for the homeless, bringing comfort to the distraught, preaching peace to those near and far. Like Jesus himself, it lives by dying, pouring out its life to satisfy human need wherever and in whatever form it finds it." [2]

It is as the servants of God that the church engages in mission. To disentangle service and mission would be an impossible task. All of the loving, compassionate acts of Jesus serve as examples for the church in its mission.

The famous prayer of Francis of Assisi expresses something of the desire of the church to be the servants of God.

O Lord, our Christ, may we have thy mind and thy spirit;
Make us instruments of Thy peace;
Where there is hatred, let us sow love;
Where there is injury, pardon;
Where there is discord, union;

Where there is doubt, faith;
Where there is despair, hope;
Where there is darkness, light;
And where there is sadness, joy.

O divine Master, grant that we may not so much seek
To be consoled, as to console;
To be understood, as to understand;
To be loved, as to love;
For it is in giving that we receive,
It is in pardoning that we are pardoned,
And it is in dying that we are born to eternal life.

The metaphors of the church abound in the New Testament. Each of the metaphors of the church can also be a metaphor for mission. But we cannot allow mission to be metaphorical; it must be actual. Mission is not simply a figure of speech, it is a method of acting in compassionate love for others.

12.
The Measure of Mission
Revelation 2—3

The National Bureau of Standards is a part of the Department of Commerce in Washington, D. C. Its task is to establish accurate measurement standards for science, industry, and commerce in the United States. All measurements in the United States, from the thrust of a rocket engine to the weight of a load of grain, depend upon the national standards kept at the Bureau.

I have read that it has a set of scales so delicate that the man who wishes to weigh something accurately must stand at least ten feet away from it lest the heat of his body upset the balance. It has been said that the balance is so delicate that it could weigh a wisp of smoke. An iron bar an inch square and a foot long is so delicately balanced that it can compute the distance that a fly lighting on one end of it can move the needle.

These give accurate measurements of physical things. But how do you measure spiritual matters? How, specifically, do you measure mission?

Jesus Christ must be the standard of measurement for both individual Christians and Christian churches. We do not measure ourselves by other persons, other institutions, other churches, or other denominations. The final measurement of mission must be computed against the life of Christ himself.

There are, however, some glimpses of churches in the New Testament that might give us some guidance in taking the measure of mission.

In Revelation 2–3 are mentioned the seven churches of Asia.

These were seven actual churches located in Asia Minor to which John wrote from the Isle of Patmos. These were not the only churches in Asia Minor. The fact that seven churches are mentioned suggests the idea of completeness. These seven churches were located in strategic places and form a circular route through the area. The letters were probably circular letters which meant that each church read the other's mail. These were representative churches and the messages were intended for all the churches of the area. Churches of today receive benefit from reading these letters to ancient churches.

Ray Summers has pointed out that a definite pattern is followed in each of the letters. The identification of Christ, the sender, is in each letter a part of the description of the glorified Christ found in the first chapter of Revelation. He claims intimate knowledge of each church. The church is commended for whatever it has of a commendable nature. He issues his complaint against the church as well as his counsel. Then he gives a promise to the faithful. The content and order may vary but the pattern follows throughout the letters.[1]

Looking at these churches from the standpoint of mission we can gain at least one dominant lesson from each church. The reaction of these churches to their opportunity can give us some indication of how we might be able to measure our effectiveness in mission.

Priority

The church at Ephesus is addressed in Revelation 2:1–7.

This church was a very active church. Doctrinally they were very sound. They could not abide the false teachings of evil men. They had patiently endured the persecution that had been directed toward them.

By opposing the compromising efforts of evil men they earned the commendation of Christ. The identity of the Nicolaitans is not definitely known. Later they were identified with the doctrine of Balaam, an Old Testament prophet. (Refer to his story in Numbers 22–24.) It can be surmised that they were people who took at least an indifferent attitude toward moral scruples. Probably, they dismissed this concern by saying that grace had ended the law.

The one complaint that the risen Christ had for the Ephesian Christians was that they had lost their first love. Still active, they went about it without the passionate concern and love which once marked their relationship to God. The sense of duty rather than the thrill of love marked their endeavors.

Love establishes priorities for us. With the love of Christ burning in the heart, the Christian is ready to give priority to mission. When that love for some reason begins to dim, then other matters, perhaps even good matters, begin to take priority. How tragic it is, but too often how true it is, that Christians will let love wane.

Operating under the impulse of love the enthusiasm for mission will continue. Priorities will be established and followed. Consider the First Baptist Church, Baton Rouge, Louisiana. Organized in 1874 with a membership of eighteen, the church now has over six thousand members. During these intervening years there have been forty-three first- and second-generation missions started by this church, thirty-four of which have developed into full time churches. Mission has maintained priority.

To a church, or a Christian, that has lost its first love the counsel of the Christ is to remember what it once experienced, repent of its action, and return to Christ. When there is the warmth and enthusiasm of love, there will be mission.

Perseverance

Perseverance was a mark of the church at Smyrna (Rev. 2:8–11). Although living in a wealthy city, the Christians evidently were poor. But they had spiritual wealth, and that is more important. To this church Christ did not offer one word of complaint.

He identified himself as the one who died and came to life. Apparently many of these Christians were facing death. But Christ stood before them as the reminder that physical death was not the end for the believer. He has the promise of eternal life.

A large group of Jews lived in Smyrna. It appears that they joined in the persecution of the Christians.

They were urged to be "faithful unto death." They later had an outstanding bishop who literally followed this admonition. In A.D. 155 Polycarp, bishop of Smyrna, was martyred. Refusing to offer a sacrifice to Caesar as god, he was given the choice of cursing the name of Christ and making sacrifice to Caesar or death. To this he replied: "Eighty and six years have I served Him and He has done me no wrong. How can I blaspheme my King who saved me?" When threatened with burning he replied: "You threaten me with the fire that burns for an hour and is speedily quenched; for you know nothing of the fire of the judgment to come and of eternal punishment which is reserved for the wicked. Why delay? Bring what you will." And Polycarp died with a prayer on his lips.

Perseverance is essential for mission. There are subtle means of inflicting difficulty and delay in mission work. Faithfulness is what Christ both demands and deserves.

Tolerance

The church at Pergamos, or Pergamum, existed in a hard place. So rampant was evil that it was called the "home of Satan" (NEB). This may have reference to its position as the administrative center of the Roman province of Asia. Caesar worship was centered there. Its letter is found in Revelation 2:12–17.

There was something to be said for these people. They had not denied the name of Christ. They had remained faithful to him when it was difficult.

But the church had one glaring weakness: it was too tolerant of evil. It was harboring heresy.

The false teaching was in the form of the Nicolaitans to which reference has already been made. Balaam had been instrumental in leading the Israelites into a compromising situation with the people who worshiped Baal. From the sound of verses 14–15 it would seem that the Nicolaitans had been guilty of loose morals and of an easy acceptance of the worship of idols by eating at their feasts. And the church had tolerated this.

Our level of tolerance has a lot to do with our sense of mission. When we accept and tolerate injustice, discrimination, hunger, poverty, and ignorance, we will likely do little to help eradicate the problem and minister to the persons. When it becomes a situation which we feel that we can no longer tolerate without at least doing something to relieve human suffering, then we will move into mission.

To the one who conquers over this broad tolerance to move into mission the Lord will give divine sustenance and a token of approval and victory inscribed with his own name.

Compromise

Thyatira (Rev. 2:18–29) was the least important of the seven cities to which these letters were sent. It has been observed that the longest letter was written to the least important city.

The church was not without virture. When the risen Christ proclaims "I know your works," it was a tender word. He knew that they had grown in grace; their latter works were better than the first. They had grown, progressed, prospered in their Christian profession.

One stark reality hovered over this, though: compromise. They had compromised with a Jezebel. Who was she? Likely she was a Jezebel-like woman who trying to lead the church into compromise with false worship and easy morality as did the original Jezebel, the wife of King Ahab. Notice that the judgment designated for her resulted from the very corruption she advocated. God still judges people according to their works.

Compromise is one of the enemies of mission. The church must stand apart from the world in which it ministers. If the church becomes too closely identified with the world, it will lose its distinctiveness. Some feel that the compromise Jezebel advocated had to do with the trade guilds whose meetings were often accompanied by sacrifice to idols and by debaucheries.

Apparently these people were not persecuted. But their life and their approach did not stand out in contrast to the society around them. Compassion, not compromise, is the stance of the believer who is concerned about mission.

Christ will triumph. And those who serve with him will be given the opportunity to share in his victory. He offers hope as bright as the morning star to guide us.

Vitality

The Sardis church (Rev. 3:1–6) seemed to be a church that was very much alive. Actually it was dead. Vance Havner tells of a prayer meeting in which a discouraged church member stated his prayer request in the presence of a visiting minister in these words: "Pray for us here. The blower is still blowing but the fire is out!"

The church had only the appearance of life. The organism had been allowed to become an organization. Plenty of activity was going on. But there was no life, no vitality to it.

When the Christ told this church, "I know your works," it was not a word of tenderness but of terror. Knowing their works the Lord knew that they were dead while having all the appearances of being alive.

But it was not too late for them. He advised: "Awake, and strengthen what remains" (Rev. 3:2, RSV). There was still hope that they could be revived and given new life.

What brings new life to a dead church? Missions. The stories could be repeated many times and in many different locations of the churches that discovered new life when they began to involve themselves in mission. Then they cease to exist for themselves in mission. Then they cease to exist for themselves and start to minister to others. They know what it means to walk with Christ on his rounds of ministry. Christ confesses that he knows those who live like him because they love like him.

Opportunity

The Christians at Philadelphia (Rev. 3:7–13) were people with an opportunity. They had before them an "open door."

For them Christ had no complaint, only praise. It had not been easy. Opportunity does not mean the absence of opposition. They had such opposition from the Jews that they were dubbed the "synagogue of Satan." Even though weak, they had not denied Christ. And before them stood an open door of mission opportunity.

Many churches have a great opportunity for mission ministry. What may seem their problem is really their possibility. Consider the downtown church that is now surrounded by high-rise apartment buildings. Once single family dwellings were located in the vicinity. They have long since gone and now the church building faces only business and apartment buildings. But how many people live in those apartments? Is it not possible that the church actually has more prospective members living within easy reach of the church than it ever did with single family dwellings? Apartments are problems; but they are also mission possibilities.

Or consider the church located in a university center. A great number of international students come to the university to study each year. The church has an opportunity to witness for Christ to these students.

Several years ago the First Baptist Church, Natchitoches, Louisiana, bought from the Roman Catholics a school and a convent whose property adjoined theirs. Northwestern State University of Louisiana is located in Natchitoches. Like many universities the dormitories at NSU are closed over the Christmas holidays. During the Christmas holidays following the purchase of this property, the vacated convent building was turned into an "International Inn" in which were housed male international students who had no place to go over the holidays. A university with its international students, as well as its American students, is an open door for mission.

The church that walks through its open door of mission opportunity is assured that it shall be a part of the sanctuary of Christ and is assured of the security of his presence.

Complacency

The saddest complaint of all is lodged against the church at Laodicea (Rev. 3:14–21). When the Lord assured them that he knew their works, it was not good. This was a complacent church. They were neither warmly on fire nor coldly unresponsive to him. They were lukewarn. Food or beverages that are lukewarm are not as tasteful as those that are either hot or cold. Neither are lukewarn churches to the Lord's liking. He indicated that since they were lukewarm he would spew them out of his mouth!

How destructive to the mission endeavor are lukewarm, complacent, self-satisfied churches! And this was just the problem at Laodicea. They had surveyed themselves and were absolutely satisfied with what they saw. Satisfied with themselves they settled into an easy, complacent existence.

The Lord was not of the same opinion, however. When he looked upon them he saw that they were "wretched, and miserable, and poor, and blind, and naked" (Rev. 3:17). Thinking that they needed nothing, they needed everything.

The problem with a self-satisfied, complacent church is that it looks exclusively inward. It looks at itself and finds itself to be finely clothed and warm. Christ counsels the church to look outward. Looking outward it can see the needs of others and can more realistically appraise its own condition. From God himself, and only from God, can come the items that give it real strength, wealth, and healing.

Christ stands at the door of each church. When admitted, he offers the most intimate of fellowship and the sharing of his power. But he never forces himself. We have the ability to open the door, from the inside, in order that we might share his life and his strength.

More than once in the letters to the seven churches of Asia churches are threatened with death and removal if they do not heed the words of the Christ. Is it possible for a church to die? Can a church fail in mission and thus lose its existence? Yes. Wayne Dehoney in his book *Set the Church Afire* cites the example of a once prosperous and prestigious church in downtown Louisville, Kentucky, that failed to recognize its responsibility. More than a quarter of a century ago Gaines S. Dobbins had conducted a survey of the church, its ministry, and its future, and had warned them that they had lost a generation. If the church was to live it would have to change its program. They did not. Today the church is gone and Baptists have now gone back into the same community to establish a mission work in the same area to reach the same people where this church once stood and failed and died.[2]

"He who has an ear, let him hear what the Spirit says to the churches" (Rev. 3:22, RSV) echoes throughout these letters. Let him hear. These words must be heeded to take the measure of mission.

Notes

Chapter 1

[1] William Barclay, *The All-Sufficient Christ* (London: SCM Press, 1963), pp. 111–112.

[2] Frank Stagg, *The Broadman Bible Commentary*, Vol. 8 (Nashville: Broadman Press, 1969), p. 175.

Chapter 3

[1] J. Wallace Hamilton, *Still the Trumpet Sounds* (Old Tappan, New Jersey: Fleming H. Revell Company, 1970), pp. 190–191.

Chapter 4

[1] Cited in A. Leonard Griffith, *God and His People* (Nashville: Abingdon Press, 1960), p. 32.

[2] Joseph B. Underwood, *By Love Compelled* (Nashville: Broadman Press, 1966), pp. 28–29.

Chapter 5

[1] Wayne Dehoney, *Set the Church Afire!* (Nashville: Broadman Press, 1971), pp. 53–55.

[2] New York: Harper and Row, 1964, p. 83.

[3] Buckner Fanning, *Christ in Your Shoes* (Nashville: Broadman Press, 1970), pp. 23–26.

[4] From the *Today's English Version* of the New Testament. Copyright © American Bible Society, 1966, 1971. All succeeding quotations from this version are indicated by the abbreviation TEV in parenthesis.

Chapter 6

[1] Samuel M. Shoemaker, *How to Become a Christian* (New York: Harper and Row, 1953), p. 74.

[2] Dallas: Evangelism Division, State Missions Commission, Baptist General Convention of Texas, 1967, p. 13.

Chapter 7
[1] Frank Pollard, "Photographer Takes Time to Care," *Baptist Standard,* September 1, 1971, p. 11.
[2] Waco, Texas: Word Inc., 1969, p. 222.
[3] From *The Gospel of John*, Volume 2, Translated and interpreted by William Barclay. Published in the U.S.A. by The Westminster Press, 1958, p. 207. Used by permission.
[4] A. Leonard Griffith, *God and His People* (Nashville: Abingdon Press, 1960), p. 67.

Chapter 8
[1] Cited in W. E. Sangster, *Sangster's Special-Day Sermons* (Nashville: Abingdon Press, 1960), p. 67.
[2] ©Copyright 1971, Broadman Press. All rights reserved. International copyright secured.
[3] *Help! I'm a Layman* (Waco, Texas: Word, Inc., 1966), p. 25.
[4] "Good Samaritan—South," *Baptist Message*, September 16, 1971, pp. 12–13.
[5] Nashville: Broadman Press, 1970, pp. 110–111.

Chapter 9
[1] *Ibid.,* pp. 9–10.
[2] Samuel M. Shoemaker, *Extraordinary Living for Ordinary Men* (Grand Rapids, Michigan: Zondervan, 1965), p. 117.

Chapter 10
[1] Nashville: Broadman Press, 1968, pp. 8–9.
[2] W. A. Criswell, "The Church of the Open Door," in Wayne Dehoney, ed., *Baptists See Black* (Waco, Texas: Word Inc., 1969), pp. 81–82.
[3] Ralph A. Langley, "Into All the World . . . of the Inner City," in Dehoney, *Baptists See Black,* pp. 70–71.
[4] Mary-Violet Burns, "Minister in a Neon Tattoed Dreamland," *Home Missions,* Vol. XLII, No. 2, February, 1971, pp. 2–6.

[5] J. Wallace Hamilton, *Where Now Is Thy God?* (Old Tappan, New Jersey: Fleming H. Revell Company, 1969), p. 32.

Chapter 11
[1] Old Tappan, New Jersey: Fleming H. Revell Company, 1965, pp. 54, 56.
[2] Nashville: Broadman Press, 1967, p. 35.

Chapter 12
[1] *Worthy Is the Lamb* (Nashville: Broadman Press, 1951), p. 108.
[2] Dehoney, *op. cit.,* pp. 98–99.